T0359617

Robert Gerrish helps people turn things they enjoy doing into a business they enjoy running. He spent his early career with a small marketing and design agency in London, becoming joint head honcho after selling to Saatchi & Saatchi Advertising in the late 1980s. After a decade as a freelance marketing man, his pursuit of a more balanced lifestyle took him to Sydney where he now lives with his wife Jane and son Jay.

In 2000 he established Flying Solo, a resource to support others going it alone. Today the community enjoys a membership of over 100,000 independent businesses. Robert co-authored his first book, the bestseller *Flying Solo: How to go it alone in business* in 2005, and it ignited his work as a presenter and advocate of all things solo. The National Library of Australia declared Flying Solo 'a site of national significance', preserving it in the Pandora web archive since 2009.

Robert sold the Flying Solo business to David Koch's Pinstripe Media Group in late 2017, and today he works as a coach and consultant to those seeking to excel as independent professionals. Alongside this he's a presenter and podcaster, and can be found online at www.robertgerrish.com.

Praise for *Flying Solo*

'. . . read this book and wake up to the possibilities.'
Michael Gerber, author of *The E-Myth* and named 'World's
Number One Small Business Guru' by *Inc.* Magazine

'. . . a breath of fresh air for anyone trapped in career hell.'
Carl Honoré, author of *In Praise of Slow* and *Under Pressure*

'Prepare to take notes!'
Dan Pink, author of *Free Agent Nation*,
A Whole New Mind and *Drive*

'A remarkable book . . . sure to fill its readers with inspiration.'
The Daily Telegraph

The

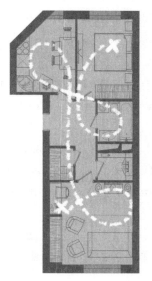

1

minute
commute

ROBERT GERRISH

MACMILLAN
Pan Macmillan Australia

Some of the people in this book have had their names changed to protect their identities.

First published 2018 in Macmillan by Pan Macmillan Australia Pty Ltd
1 Market Street, Sydney, New South Wales, Australia, 2000

Copyright © Robert Gerrish 2018

The moral right of the author to be identified as the author of this work has been asserted.

All rights reserved. No part of this book may be reproduced or transmitted by any person or entity (including Google, Amazon or similar organisations), in any form or by any means, electronic or mechanical, including photocopying, recording, scanning or by any information storage and retrieval system, without prior permission in writing from the publisher.

Cataloguing-in-Publication entry is available
from the National Library of Australia
http://catalogue.nla.gov.au

Typeset in 13/17 pt Minion Pro by Midland Typesetters, Australia
Printed by McPherson's Printing Group
Cover design and internal design features by Lisa White

The author and the publisher have made every effort to contact copyright holders for material used in this book. Any person or organisation that may have been overlooked should contact the publisher.

MIX
Paper from
responsible sources
FSC® C001695
www.fsc.org

The paper in this book is FSC® certified.
FSC® promotes environmentally responsible,
socially beneficial and economically viable
management of the world's forests.

To my artist wife Jane who floods family life
with love, creativity and quirkiness, and to our
wonderful son Jay who will soon put it all to work.

Contents

Contents

Contents

Introduction

'Life isn't about finding yourself. Life is about creating yourself.'

Aficionados of George Bernard Shaw, to whom this quote is attributed, doubt he ever muttered such words, as he wasn't known for penning inspirational quotes.

There's really quite a kerfuffle about the topic if you care to search the web, but I wouldn't bother. Frankly I couldn't care less and nor should you.

Since starting my solo business journey some thirty years ago, I've realised it's not about where we get our inspiration or who provides it; what matters is what we do with it.

With *The 1 Minute Commute*, I aim to inspire you. You may be searching for inspiration to make the leap into your own business or you may need motivation to keep going.

Either way *The 1 Minute Commute* will help. Let me tell you why I wanted to write it.

By my mid-thirties, I'd helped build and grow a marketing and design agency in London and had played a part in selling it to Saatchi & Saatchi Advertising. With my little Mercedes sports and a detached house in leafy West London, I may have appeared to the outside world to be vaguely successful.

In truth, I was a shallow, egotistical twit, full of my own importance, with a life largely devoid of meaning and purpose.

Yes, I was well suited to the advertising industry.

It took the premature death of my wonderful father, and shortly thereafter my darling mother, to realise something needed to change, lest I too keel over as a consequence of stress, pressure or a poorly dealt hand.

Footloose, fancy-free and still more than a little arrogant, I quit my flashy job, gave all my worldly goods to friends and charity shops and, armed with a round-the-world ticket, set off in search of myself.

It was never going to work.

A year later, with a swathe of well-thumbed Lonely Planet guide books and a stack of stories that no-one has ever wanted to hear, I stumbled into a job in Sydney, as general manager of a biggish design group.

I'd traded a big job in London for a big job in Sydney. Big deal.

This was the mid-1990s and a change was in the air in the world of work. As I wrote a few years ago in my first book, *Flying Solo: How to go it alone in business*, the number of sole traders, free-lancers and free agents was exploding and Australia was uniquely placed to spearhead the concept of a 'lifestyle business'. A lifestyle where my commute was from the kitchen to the study, and I could dip in and out of being 'at work' and 'at home' at a moment's notice.

I wanted a piece of that: a vocation designed around the way I chose to live. I wanted it so badly that I quit my silly job and got to work.

'The future isn't a place you'll go; it's a place you'll invent.'

Nancy Duarte

Of course I also needed to eat, particularly as I'd taken on the added responsibility of being a husband and a new father.

With the support and encouragement of my wife Jane, I consulted to small, creative businesses, helping them get their marketing right and ensuring the right people were in the right jobs. Alongside this I helped change nappies and devoured every book, course and presentation I could lay my hands on that explored new ways of working.

One such resource was Mihaly Csikszentmihalyi's 2004 TED talk, which explored finding pleasure and lasting satisfaction in activities that bring about a state of 'flow' – that feeling that what you're doing is precisely what you should be doing.

For me the signs that I was indeed answering my 'calling' came thick and fast, and if you follow the steps outlined in *The 1 Minute Commute*, I'll wager it will for you too.

As part of my 'professional development', I trained to be a coach and (in case anyone is impressed) became one of the first people in Australasia to obtain International Coach Federation accreditation.

Actually I'm not fussed whether you're impressed or not because ABC Television was, and chose me to feature in a *Four Corners* segment on new work practices. So there.

Overnight my fledgling business-coaching practice went nuts. But as fast as the money rolled in, calm and balance slipped away.

What a dilemma. I'd found that thing I really wanted to do, but was more overworked and overwhelmed than ever.

And then I remembered I knew a bit about marketing and positioning.

Most importantly, as I talk about at length in *The 1 Minute Commute*, I realised that you can charge more and do your best work when you surround yourself with ideal clients.

Up to this point, I mistakenly thought anyone with a heartbeat and credit card was a good fit. Wrong, wrong, wrong.

Within days, I'd fired most of my customers, registered 'Flying Solo' and started what became Australia's largest online community of little businesses.

Throughout *The 1 Minute Commute*, I'll introduce you to members of that community, sharing their many valuable insights and lessons, and I'll set you tasks and assignments that I've found useful on my journey.

I hope that *The 1 Minute Commute* can signal the start of your journey, or perhaps the rejuvenation of one that's begun. Please think of this as a *workbook* and don't be precious. Scribble in it, draw in it, fold down pages*. Really make it your own. Come back to it time and time again, like a user manual.

Life is about creating yourself. As someone said.

---

* Library copies excluded.

1.

Why Work Solo?

Joining the soloism movement

Why do so many people dream of working for themselves?

There are lots of reasons. The big one, though, is that you can be so creative with your career. Work your own hours, on your own terms, on projects you care about, with clients you choose.

You get to shape your professional life to accommodate all areas of your personal life – family, health or travel. Not to mention a one-minute commute (if that!). In short, it's about flexibility and control.

Now that's pretty attractive. Who wouldn't want this?

However, with all that freedom and choice, it can be hard to know where to start, and what steps to take. Fear not, I'm here to share the blueprint for going it alone.

But first, what exactly is a soloist? Is it the same as a small-business owner? Are they entrepreneurs or freelancers? Well, there's crossover, for sure, so let's untangle it.

In the context of this book, a soloist is someone going it alone in business – working for themselves and by themselves. The term solopreneur is also common, as is one I particularly like, independent professional. Officially, you might call yourself a sole trader . . . but few people use this term out loud – it's more something for your tax return!

As a soloist, the success, prosperity, enjoyment and workload is all down to one person: YOU!

So does this mean that you have to do everything? Thankfully not. In this book I'll explain how to avoid getting overwhelmed, and lots of other common pitfalls along the way.

Some soloists start out with the intention of growing bigger, but research undertaken at Flying Solo revealed that over two-thirds are happy staying small . . . so long as they're nice and profitable.

What about the distinction between a soloist and a freelancer?

Many see themselves as freelancers – the very term has a nice energy, thanks to the 'free' bit, and the majority fit the soloist definition I've just outlined. On the other hand, some 'freelancers' are heavily reliant on just one client: a former employer perhaps.

Typically freelancers respond to work opportunities or 'gigs' that are advertised, throwing their hat in the ring in the hope of scoring the job.

In many cases, though, they're competing against others

with a lower cost of living, or a model that's simply not as reliant on income – maybe a student just trying to get some experience. Such a scenario can become a 'race to the bottom' in pricing terms.

From a client's perspective, sourcing workers this way may look financially attractive, but can be messy with the endless back and forth, deviations from the brief, compromises galore and a keen lesson in the nature of false economies.

In my view, freelancing is a way of work. Soloism is a way of life.

Soloists create their own opportunities, build long-term relationships and determine their own fees, and in this book I'll show you how to do just that.

Let's look at entrepreneurs. While the term is used liberally, I think of an entrepreneur as an individual who has their sights set firmly on growth, scale and exit – i.e. get it going, build it, sell it off and get started on the next one.

Can a soloist be an entrepreneur? Of course, and there's a strong air of entrepreneurial spirit in many solo businesses.

But from research within the solo community, I can tell you that the majority tend to be people who are in their business for the long haul. In many cases they've designed it as a distinct lifestyle choice. And if you're loving what you do and it allows you to live where and how you like, why would you want to stop?

When I talk about 'lifestyle' and 'business' in the same sentence, the last thing I want to conjure up is the typical stock-photo image of beautiful people lazing in hammocks slung between palm trees, laptop between their knees and a speedboat tethered in the distance.

In my view, a 'lifestyle business' can be defined as one that while making money has as its primary purpose the need to support the business owner's desired lifestyle. That might be a business that allows frequent travel or the ability to be location-independent or to be more present for kids and family or indeed just to be working at a less hectic pace.

Most soloists are running a 'lifestyle business', and in this book I'll show you how to join them.

What type of soloist are you?

I'm often asked to describe a typical soloist. But the reality is that soloists come from every walk of life, are just as likely to be male as female, and the demographic spread is broad.

Certainly a large percentage are what I think of as 'independent professionals'; that is those working in a largely consultative role, often selling their professional services. For what it's worth, these days this is how I think of myself.

Soloists are strongly represented across all industries and sectors, including, but definitely not limited to the following:

- Business consultants
- Advisors and coaches
- Retailers
- Life coaches
- Artists
- Virtual assistants
- Designers
- Website developers
- Property developers

- Writers
- Editors
- Photographers
- Videographers
- Tradespeople
- Health professionals
- Cleaners
- Landscapers
- Finance specialists
- Bookkeepers
- Architects
- Digital marketers
- Real estate agents.

And the list goes on and on . . . This is great news, because no matter what your skills, you'll discover a mass of opportunities and options for running your own solo business.

Let's dig deeper into the different ways you might beat a path to soloism.

Born soloists

These are people with innate talents; for example: athletes, artists, writers, performers, actors, singers, musicians and so on. You get the idea.

Many recognise their abilities at an early age and quickly answer to their calling. The pull factor is so compelling, it's like they have no other option.

For most of us, though, the path to soloism is not so clear-cut and while the destination may be similar, the journey is quite different.

Soloists by design

This is the group who deliberately pursue a career as an independent. A broad range make up this category, including 'corporate escapees' pursuing their passions, and fresh-faced graduates who've never worked for anybody else and aren't the least bit attracted to what their parents would consider a conventional career path.

Accidental soloists

Another large group are the 'accidental soloists'. An accidental soloist often feels the decision to go solo has been made for them. They haven't sought soloism out, but rather it's found them. When asked to explain how they got to where they are, the answer is typically something like, 'Oh, you know, I sort of fell into it.' Fate has played a large part in proceedings for the accidental soloist.

The impetus might have been something as simple as a friend's off-the-cuff remark, 'Oh, I love that jewellery you made for my birthday. Have you ever thought about making it for a living?' Such a comment may spark the decision to fly solo.

Circumstantial soloists

Typically the people in this group will have held a traditional job in the past before experiencing a life change that motivated them to go it alone.

A large proportion of this group are new parents who want the flexibility to base themselves from home to be with their children. Others may have been called on to care for an elderly relative, or perhaps their children have flown the nest and they seek a less career-driven life path.

Keen to maintain their professional identity and income, but dismayed by the inflexibility of traditional work culture, circumstances drive this group to start their own business to carve out a new way of working and living.

Once again, flexibility is the key motivator and benefit of going it alone. For them, as for many, soloism offers the best of both worlds.

Unpleasant experiences such as retrenchment or career burnout can also accelerate the move to soloism. While such soloists may have never seriously considered the option of their own business until circumstances forced the issue, soloism can often become the silver lining to a mid-life cloud.

While circumstances do sometimes fall in your favour, the chances of you realising your ambitions are far greater if you face up to the challenge of engineering your solo journey for yourself, an ambition that I'm delighted to report has never been more culturally acceptable or accessible than it is today.

Banishing myths and outmoded thinking

While the idea of being the architect of your own venture is increasingly popular, the traditional work culture can be hard to shake when creating your own business. Old-school thinking can mess with your head and put the brakes on your progress!

So let's banish some assumptions and create some new realities.

Myth: Get more done by working long hours

One old assumption you're sure to be familiar with is the notion that you have to work all hours to achieve success. The very idea that the *time* you spend *at* work is more important than the *quality* of the work you do is utterly crazy. It positions one person as 'committed' and the other as a 'slacker' regardless of what they produce.

Never mind that the one working long hours feels permanently wiped out, hates the work and is not good company to be around!

You're probably familiar with the notion of 'facetime' or 'presenteeism' – where a person arrives at the office super early or stays late simply because it looks good. Fortunately, soloists have no reason to subscribe to this kind of nonsense.

As a soloist, I invite you to abandon the notion that you work like a dog all week and recover on the weekends. In soloism, you design your week, work the hours you choose and balance your day as you see fit. Productivity is the focus, not facetime.

Myth: Work is all about money

Another old assumption has to do with enjoyment:

'*Work is just something you have to do to pay the bills.*'

Rubbish!

Most of us spend more of our time working than we do with friends and family, and when work's such a massive part of our life, we surely owe it to ourselves to find a vocation that can be enjoyed.

Happily, going it alone enables you to do just that. And if you're not passionate about what you're doing, well, do something else. Maybe that's why you're here?

Myth: Real work happens in real offices

What about the idea that you have to work in an office to be serious? Ha! Technology has surely buried this one once and for all, and rightly so. Sounds to me like language used by those trying to reassure themselves that their long commute is worthwhile!

Believe me when I say that you can conduct your business from wherever you like. Your home, your garden, a café, a co-working space, anywhere.

Don't go signing any office leases just yet!

Myth: Working by yourself is lonely

Another myth is that soloism is a lonely and isolating pursuit. I'm here to tell you that with a little planning, it needn't be.

There's a very healthy community of soloists you can connect with both in your neighbourhood and online. Make the effort to participate and you'll reap the rewards in more ways than you can imagine.

You can find new clients, discuss business ideas, share advice, and generally enjoy connecting with people like you. Soloism has rekindled the master/apprentice kind of relationship, with mentoring and idea sharing among independents being very common.

You may be working solo, but you're definitely not alone.

Myth: Bigger is better

A bigger business being a better business is another myth. It amazes me that this thinking prevails even with so many corporate scandals, collapses, executive excesses, and behaviour that benefits shareholders but not employees or the environment.

Technology has drastically levelled the playing field so us little guys have the tools we need to take on the big guys, particularly in the areas of communication, accounting and marketing.

Many organisations now choose to work with independent specialists. Unburdened by bureaucracy, we have the added advantage of agility, speed, quality and competitive price.

Myth: Work hard now, enjoy life later

'Work hard now, enjoy life later.'

This one's the worst old-school myth of the lot, in my view.

It didn't work out well for my father and it's not a way of thinking my son will inherit from me. Instead I hope to show my son how to live in the present and enjoy life's journey to the full.

No doubt we all know people who postponed their happiness for a day that never came. Enjoyment simply must be a part of now.

MYTHBUSTER

Which of these myths do you need to drag to the trash?

Watch out for family and friends!

Getting started is not without challenges, but I tell you what, it would be a whole lot easier without the band of naysayers all around you – those seemingly trying to scare the hell out of you. Including a few that may reside in your own head.

'You're really sure you want to do this?'
'Do you have enough money?'
'Why don't you get a job?'
'Why don't you stay in the job you've got?'
'Do you know how many small businesses fail?'
'You'll be working all day and all night, you know!'

And on and on and on.

These 'helpful' questions and horror stories are likely flooding in from your friends, family and work colleagues, and the result is an undermining of your confidence and your desire to get started.

What's really happening here? Why do people say these things? Of course such comments may well be driven by a genuine and well-founded concern – or it could be that you're destabilising their nice, comfortable equilibrium. You might be threatening their place in the world. Your courage might challenge their weakness.

Here's what to do: quietly sit and listen. Be friendly. Be graceful. Acknowledge their concerns and say, 'Thank you.' 'Thank you for your advice.' 'Thank you for your valuable input.' Show your confidence; demonstrate your commitment.

Afterwards, carefully and thoroughly check your plans and reassure yourself you've got the areas in question covered. By so doing you'll further embrace the positive change you're making and, if after closer scrutiny your plans still stack up, you'll strengthen your resolve. The more robust your belief, the better able you'll be to weather the naysayers and the more likely your ultimate success.

I rather like Dropbox founder Drew Houston's take on the topic:

'Don't worry about failure; you only have to be right once.'

In Flying Solo's 2016–2017 survey of over 1000 soloists, respondents reported being happier than they anticipated; more positive, more fulfilled, more confident, more decisive, more accepting and more community-minded. They gleefully report that they're nicer people to be around and for those with children, they are more engaged as parents.

They feel healthier, more balanced, calmer and get better sleep. Unbelievable? Well, believe it.

When is the right time to launch?

When will you know it's time to make the leap? Good question. I can tell you there will simply never be a day when you cross the last task off your list and say, 'Great! That's all done, time to work for myself.'

'The way to get started is to quit talking and begin doing.'

Walt Disney had it about right. Countless people have a burning desire to start something of their own, but they have a host of perfectly logical reasons why next year or the year after that will be the ideal time.

Don't get me wrong; rigorous questioning is necessary

and healthy. But overthinking can be your enemy. I see lots of people waiting for the 'perfect' time to get going, and then putting a stack of impossible conditions in place:

> *'I'll wait until I know x, until I've saved y, until my work situation eases, until I get my partner's approval.'*

You have to recognise that there will in fact never be an ideal time, at some point, you just have to shout 'Geronimo'.
Corporate copywriter Jim Lee sums it up nicely:

> *'It was a case of acting on that nagging feeling of if I never gave it a go, I would regret it for the rest of my life. Now it's a case of "If only I'd done it sooner"!'*

Let's take a look at some of the excuses . . . sorry, I mean some of the reasons people delay.

The first is that 'you're just not quite ready'. Have you ever seen a baby take its first steps? Not a hundred per cent ready, but ready enough to give it a go. Will she fall over? Very likely yes. Will she get straight up and try again? Damn right. Each time she gets a little further on until she's off and running.

'The design just needs a little finessing.' No, it doesn't. After a career in the marketing and design industry, I knew how important detail was. I was used to everything having to be perfect.

Thankfully, when starting my solo venture, a friend who knew my history saw what was going on and called me out on it: 'Just get started,' she screamed at me. I did, and so should you.

I like the way author Liz Gilbert puts it:

'Perfection is fear in high heels.'

'The market isn't ready.' Really? What did Henry Ford famously say?

'If I'd asked people what they wanted, they would have said a faster horse.'

Similarly, the audience's readiness was in severe doubt by those surrounding Steve Jobs when he was on the cusp of giving the world 'a thousand songs in your pocket'.

There's no denying that doing research to ensure there's a market is essential, but when you've done your research, when you've set out your vision and path: Just. Get. Going.

A note of caution: no matter how much planning, research or forecasting you do, you *will* underestimate the time it takes to build revenue. I've worked alongside a heap of solo start-ups and it can take longer than you think to get things moving. But it's worth the wait.

If you've got a full-time job now, consider starting your solo enterprise in your spare time while keeping a salary. Or drop a day or two in order to maintain some sound, regular income.

It can be hard work for sure – with a few late nights and weekend work – but it's a way that you can keep your day job and follow your dream at the same time.

Starting up alongside other work is also a great way to test and modify your offering. Are people interested? Is there the demand you predicted? Is the price right? Who's your competition? What marketing channels are available?

You can discover all this before you've even thought about quitting your day job. Whether you decide to transition slowly or dive in with both feet, starting a solo business with immediate or early financial pressure is not ideal.

Do a thorough review of all your outgoings, set yourself a strict budget while you build up your earnings and keep some reserves, a buffer.

For photographer Tricia Bello, her initial launch into soloism was very much a 'work-in-progress':

> *'When I decided to start, I had half a plan, the rest was winging it or flying by the seat of my pants! I've had fun and stressful moments, almost gave up once. But I'm still going and slowly (as I learn new things) remodelling my ideas and plans! And taking tiny steps closer to success!'*

A child taking those first steps needs some soft cushions around for a while.

WHAT'S HOLDING YOU BACK?

If you have fears that are causing you to hesitate, jot them down. Keep them to hand as you work through *The 1 Minute Commute* and enjoy crossing them out as your concern subsides. If anything remains on the list, we should talk!

2.

What You Need to Succeed

What makes a successful soloist?

It's pretty easy to recognise the characteristics that practically guarantee solo success, but don't panic if you don't recognise yourself in the portrait I'm about to paint.

I don't know anyone who has every element in place at the outset. In fact one of the main things is being able to assess the risk and make the leap in spite of a few gaps.

At this point the key is to keep building the picture of where you're heading in terms of your own growth and development.

Successful soloists can because they think they can

Anything you do on your own demands a level of self-confidence. An underlying sense that 'I've got this' is going to help move your business forward.

The reason going solo is a popular option among an older demographic like mine is that by now we tend to know who we are and what we want in life, both traits that underpin successful solo careers.

But regardless of age, if you're inquisitive, hungry for personal growth and on a mission to deepen your understanding of yourself and others, you and soloism will get along just fine.

Soloists push for authenticity and integrity in all they do, and work to keep in touch with those things that are important in their lives: their values.

As a result, what they do fits closely with who they are, which in turn creates a need to express their personality through their work, keeping them happy and motivated.

Successful soloists rank happiness and fulfilment very highly! Well above money and power.

Successful soloists are savvy with marketing principles

Marketing can seem like an overwhelming and scary concept for some, but if you are interested in how people tick and curious to understand why consumers do what they do, you'll reveal a knack for sales and marketing that you may not even realise you had.

Successful soloists show the hallmarks of a smart marketer by focusing on the needs of those they are delivering to: their clients and prospects. They listen intently and develop genuine empathy with them, and then they figure out how best they can help.

In this way, the product or service offered represents the best possible match between what they can provide and what the market wants. Success at sales and marketing is not about pushing, but about responding well to needs and offering great pre-sales service.

Successful soloists love their work

As a soloist, you can align what you do with who you are. When you've done this, it's relatively straightforward to maintain a healthy passion for your work. After all, when you turn up to the work space you've chosen, to do work you've chosen with people you've chosen, what's not to love?

The challenge, though, is not to rest on your laurels; it's healthy to keep an eye on your personal evolution. To that end, successful soloists position themselves firmly in the flow of new ideas, influences and information, which of course adds to skills and knowledge and helps refine their offering.

Gradually, they grow their expertise, which boosts confidence and helps with standing up and speaking up.

As we'll explore later in *The 1 Minute Commute*, once you get to recognise the value of *your* opinions, you'll feel more compelled to engage in one-on-one conversations, article writing, blogging, social media and on and on and on!

But I'm getting ahead of myself, a sure sign that I love *my* work and am easily excited!

Successful soloists are natural connectors

Successful soloists never miss an opportunity for matchmaking. At networking events, for example, they say things like, 'You're an illustrator? I met an author earlier looking for an illustrator. Let's try to find her.' More introverted types may be inclined to connect people virtually instead. Either way, though, soloists get a kick out of bringing people together.

This of course creates a positive reverse flow of opportunities, not only in the form of additional business, but in improved personal reputation trust. Soloists create virtuous circles, where their generous actions return in their favour.

And this characteristic helps get the ear of influential people because they aren't afraid to approach them, whether for a friendly chat or to seek advice, because they are not intimidated by traditional hierarchies or status.

Successful soloists don't put people on pedestals. They think the best of others, preferring to be trusting not cynical, optimistic not pessimistic.

When you're a successful soloist, usually your expectations will be reinforced because you'll tend to attract and engage with people with the same open and upbeat attitude.

Successful soloists don't make excuses

You'll never hear any dog-ate-my-homework defensiveness or sob stories from a successful soloist. Instead, successful soloists face up to their mistakes, seek to make amends and put processes in place to prevent the error from reoccurring. Faced with criticism, they will keep a cool head and not take the words personally; instead they'll embrace the 'learning' opportunity.

Soloists don't blame things like their lack of wealth or a tough upbringing for when things don't go their way.

Successful soloists collaborate

Successful soloists are open to collaboration with anyone, even competitors. Instead of working *against* others, successful soloists view those in the same field as potential colleagues – people to learn from and be inspired by.

It's far better to be energised and motivated by the activity of others than allow it to get under your skin and have you hiding under your desk!

I remember a couple of years ago, a colleague of mine was annoyed to see some of his work effectively being plagiarised by 'competitors'. Rather than go into attack mode though, he did his research, saw they were misguided more than malicious and ended up signing them up as affiliates. What started out as potentially upsetting ended up as an income generator!

It's helpful to have healthy relationships with those in your industry, as they may be able to help shoulder some work during a busy period, cover you while you're on holiday and share information relevant to your industry. And of course ideally, this collaborator will do just the same for you.

Successful soloists cherish their independence

Not every soloist has been the best employee and many could never and would never go back to 'working for the man'. In their pre-solo days, many had difficulties settling down in one job and roamed from role to role like professional nomads.

Their need for autonomy can make it hard for other people to manage and motivate them. Luckily, if this sounds like you, working for yourself is the ideal opportunity to flex your independence. Freedom is arguably soloism's biggest reward, but, and this is critical, it does entail self-discipline.

Successful soloists have to be able to work in the absence of a formal structure and put their heads down. If they're insufficiently grounded or organised, nothing gets done and the business collapses.

Successful soloists are good with money

It's crucial to be (again) 'disciplined' with money, particularly in the early days when workflow and income can be sporadic. In no small way, soloists are essentially backing themselves, but they are willing to make financial sacrifices when necessary. In fact, many soloists master the art of being happy with less money, because for them the pursuit of it comes at the expense of the balanced lifestyle they cherish.

While the pursuit of riches is important for some, for others, financial stability is the aim of the game. This may not be as sexy or ambitious-sounding, but I can tell you it's what soloists want.

So the soloists I consider to be the most successful have the courage to make up their own measures of success, often rejecting traditional benchmarks like material wealth and social status in favour of the freedom to work their own hours and the opportunity to express themselves through their work.

Successful soloists know their priorities

Emotional stability is an intrinsic part of solo success, and it is important to support yourself and receive support from friends and family. Rather than worshipping at the altar of work, successful soloists take care of their core needs by nurturing relationships and prioritising their health.

Many will seek opportunities for personal development and

strive to avoid endless work domination, although good self-care means they have plenty in the tank for those times they need to go hard in their work. Generally, though, they believe in balance, pacing themselves, a holistic outlook and commitment to their wellbeing.

Freelancer Sandy Markson has clearly got the idea:

'I say no when a client's need will mean exhausting hours and hassle for me. It's certainly not that I don't need the money. It's just that now I've got my priorities sorted around my needs.'

Successful soloists keep their cool
In the face of stressful situations, it never helps to freak out. When soloists are under pressure they take responsibility for the situation; they're aware enough to recognise issues and creative enough to solve them.

Successful soloists are doers
Successful soloists convert words into action. They don't merely pay lip service to their plans, *saying* they'll do it; they actually take the necessary steps to get their show on the road.

Some people procrastinate at the planning stage of a new business or project. They will try to mitigate risk by poring over detailed plans that attempt to anticipate every possible outcome. But there's no such thing as the 'perfect plan' and those dedicated to creating one are, consciously or not, employing a stalling technique.

While plans are important and I don't advocate 'seat of the pants' as a strategy, there's no denying that allowing for the 'dynamics of change' trumps any path that is too prescribed.

You're going to need to have the courage to face ambiguities and take the plunge in spite of them.

Constant change and uncertainty are one of the few guarantees in soloville. But having the freedom to be reactive and spontaneous is one of the great joys.

Successful soloists are courageous
Finally, those who nail soloism appreciate the importance of facing the future head-on to take control of their destiny.

Take this on board, and you too can begin to guide your circumstances in a specific direction, rather than have them guide you any old where.

Don't worry. No-one has every characteristic I've covered, and no-one is expecting you to be superhuman. Doubts and negative feelings are inevitably an occasional companion on your journey.

If I've succeeded in rattling, exciting and maybe causing you to pause and think deeply about what it takes to succeed, then my work here is done!

CHARACTER ASSIGNATION!

Looking briefly at the attributes of solo success, circle the three that most need your attention:

Positive thinker / Marketing savvy / Lover of work / Natural connector / Self-accountable / Strong collaborator / Cherish independence / Good with money / Courageous / Conscious of priorities / Cool headed / I get things done

3.

Design Your Workspace

How to choose where you work

Many soloists work from a home base; while that is nirvana for some, it can be hell on earth for others. The term 'home office' is extremely broad. It can mean a cramped desk at the end of the bed for some, or an inspiring dedicated office space for others.

The most important piece of advice I have on this topic is to take the time and thought to give yourself the very best working environment you can. Start by choosing the best possible space available.

Don't just plonk yourself in the kitchen or the worst room in the house if you can help it, because you'll likely be spending more time awake here than anywhere else. Do whatever you can to set yourself up in an inspiring spot – somewhere with good light and ideally a pleasant outlook.

While an office with a view may sound like a recipe for a distracted mind, the opposite is true. It turns out that access to sunlight boosts productivity.

In a study by the California Energy Commission, workers who sat near a window performed better, processing work up to 12 per cent faster and performing up to 25 per cent better on tests on mental function and memory recall. That's pretty good!

Ideally, keep your workspace out of your main bedroom. A desk at the end of the bed is really not a good idea. It can interrupt your sleep and impact how you feel about your work and life.

For years I worked in a shed in our garden. It was a tiny space, but it was quiet, had a nice outlook and worked really well. Be a bit creative when you think about your space . . . and of course it's okay to mix things up.

Mixing things up is precisely what my good friend Kate Toon, an SEO consultant, trainer and author, did. Here's the solution she created:

'My husband and I both work from home and used to share an office. Sometimes it was nice to have him with me all day. But generally we annoyed the crap out of each other, and I often even found the sound of his breathing irritating.

'I'm incredibly proud of the end result of the cabin, or Tooncave as I've taken to calling it. It really has become my happy place. This was a big investment in me. But after five years of scrabbling around working in cafés, the kitchen and a cramped office, I felt I deserved it. It feels like a celebration of my success to date.

26

'And my husband and I are feeling the benefit of not working so closely together. It's nice to commute across the lawn and meet him for dinner.'

These days I work two days in my city office, two days in my home office and then on the fifth day I have what I think of as some nomadic time. On this day I may head to my local library, as I find it the perfect place when I'm in writing mode, or I've got some hand-picked cafés that I spend a bit of time in.

You might want to have a look at co-working spaces; many offer free trial days. Having others around you can help give you a sense of connection. If you like the company but not the background noise of a co-working space, a good set of headphones with music or 'white noise' helps focus.

By contrast a friend of mine prefers to work from home, but finds it helpful to have radio chat shows playing on low volume in the background.

If I need to ponder a problem or do some creative thinking, I'll take myself off for a walk and record my thoughts on my phone as I go.

There's nothing wrong with establishing yourself in a space at home and settling in there for the duration. But you can also be a bit more playful and creative.

I know a soloist PR consultant who every couple of months just gets on a train for the day with her laptop. Two hours one way, two hours back, with lunch and a walk in the middle. Lots of yummy thinking time and ever-changing scenery. Small wonder she loves it!

Give yourself permission to be inventive with how and where you work. This is your business, your work style. You get to choose, so don't be afraid to try new things.

The important point here is to make a conscious choice about where you work. Be purposeful and flexible – where you work this week can be different next week. Don't be afraid to mix things up.

The most productive environment

While many believe that creativity blooms from chaos, the truth is that for most of us a disordered office won't help us get work done.

A Harvard Business Review study found that a clean desk helps you stick with a task for more than one and a half times longer. So, while it may feel like organised mess, you're likely sitting in the middle of an obstacle to your productivity.

Workspaces can become magnets for clutter: unorganised files, unread books, reminders, stationery, receipts and overflowing inboxes, physical and virtual. All this really does is remind us of what's unfinished; what we've yet to do.

And they are all temptations for procrastination. Even if you don't think you're noticing the mess, your subconscious is weighed down by disarray, which impacts your focus.

By contrast, facing a clean and tidy workspace encourages consistency and persistence, and reduces frustration and fatigue. Start by clearing your desk, then make a commitment to keep it organised each day.

But what's most important is how your workspace makes you feel. Is it inviting, inspiring and motivating, or the opposite? Layout, colour and lighting all need careful consideration. Given you'll be spending so much time in it, building a business you love, it's crucial that it works for you.

Get the layout right

I loosely follow the Chinese philosophy of feng shui – which focuses on the harmonisation between people, buildings and objects. It's a great philosophy to delve into, as the principles make a world of difference to how you feel about your surroundings and indeed how your surroundings feel.

Try not to have a door behind you when you work as it's shown to be unsettling to the mind when you can't see who's coming; avoid proximity to busy thoroughfares as these bring noise pollution and negativity to your space.

When it comes to office furniture, a desk or work surface where you can spread out effectively creates a canvas for the work that needs to get your attention.

Have plenty of room for storage and good lighting, and don't skimp on a good supportive chair, it's definitely worth the investment. Far better to have a good-quality ergonomic chair like the classic Herman Miller Aeron or similar, even if it's second-hand, than to settle for something that doesn't give you support.

In terms of visual decoration, you might like to decorate with art, a rug or plants. Maybe photos of loved ones, or inspiring quotes. This is your space, your business. Do it your way.

What about fragrances? Many soloists talk of the positive impact of burning oils or candles, even having fresh flowers if they're in your budget (or your garden). I can't underestimate the power of creating a workspace that you really love being in.

Sitting or standing?

In the last few years I've started working regularly at a stand-up desk and have found that it's boosted my energy and helped my posture and wellbeing. Studies have shown that if men sit six hours or more a day we have a life expectancy that's up to 20 per cent shorter than those who sit for three hours or less. For women, it's even worse: a 40 per cent shorter life expectancy!

And I'm sorry to tell you that nothing cancels out the effects of sitting for long hours, not even frequent gym workouts, long walks or yoga.

When you sit slumped in your chair, your metabolism drops, calorie-burning slows . . . and the risk of obesity and diabetes increases. The American Cancer Society found that those who stand for a quarter of the day dramatically reduce their chance of obesity.

So for me, standing is a part of how I work. I prefer to stand for specific actions – clearing email, talking on the phone, creating mind maps and action lists and recording podcast interviews. Detailed writing I do sitting down. Bookkeeping I do sitting down.

Specially made stand-up desks are becoming more widely available but can still be costly. Fortunately more economical options do exist. My first iteration of a stand-up 'desk' was simply a tall table where I perched my laptop. Now I've a set-up that converts from stand to sit at the touch of a button.

If you're not keen on the stand-up desk idea, promise me you won't spend hours on end sitting down. It's bad for productivity, morale, your body and your soul. Instead, set a timer to go off every forty minutes and walk around or have a stretch.

Just a small but regular amount of activity can make a big difference to your long-term health.

Let's talk ergonomics

It may not sound sexy, but ergonomics are super important. Often a few tweaks to your current set-up will be all you need to prevent injury.

For example, an external monitor or laptop stand can help prevent pain in the neck. An external keyboard helps keep repetitive strain injury at bay. Make sure you have your monitor at the right height and keep your shoulders relaxed rather than hunched.

While sitting, your elbows and knees should pretty well be at right angles and of course your back well supported.

Sound pollution

Finally, give some thought to sound pollution, whether from outside or family members, notably the kids! My home office is completely soundproofed. When I moved in, my son was very young and it was important to me to be able to concentrate on my work without his interruptions or occasional tantrum.

It might sound harsh now, but when I built my office, I set the doorhandles high out of my young toddler son's reach.

Boundaries only work when people know about them. Particularly little people!

MY SPACE

Capture your first thoughts on the components of your ideal workspace. Words or scribbles are fine.

Embrace the fully nomadic life

One of the many possibilities soloism brings is the option to work from anywhere for an indefinite period. Indeed, with the right business model and design, many have the freedom to be totally nomadic – travelling the world working in different cities each week.

In reality though, not every soloist can or wants to adopt the full-on life of a nomad. Little things like face-to-face customers, children, schools, partners and family can kind of get in the way.

But, lots of soloists do enjoy the flexibility to work away from their home, office, shop or workshop, even for short periods . . . so let's look at how to go about doing just that.

First thing is getting really clear on what equipment you need to have with you so that you can operate your business efficiently and effectively in a mobile format.

For a good number of individuals and certainly for me when I was full-time in my coaching business, if I felt I needed a change of scene it was very easy to up sticks and work pretty well from any location. All I needed was my laptop and good internet access, and I was ready to roll.

I could keep all my client-report forms online, access my calendar, do all my banking and invoicing; in short, I could carry on with my work regardless of location and my income didn't dip at any point.

Indeed for many of our holidays, when our son was young, I was able to just take my laptop with me, find a quiet corner in whatever holiday apartment we were in and carry on generating income and working in my business.

And for a number of soloists – particularly in the professional services side of things: writers, designers, coaches, consultants and so on – it can be easy to have a mobile business and is very attractive to do so. And that's not to say it doesn't take work to get it right, as publisher, co-parent and home-schooling advocate Grace Okeke told me.

> 'We have just been on a tropical island for three weeks, and are now living for eight weeks in provincial France. So in that respect, working for ourselves has been amazing.
>
> 'Changes that have been slower to come have been working out a work–life balance that suits us, and means we're still highly productive, but also have ample time to spend with our son. Without childcare, this is still very much in progress and we're definitely not happy with the balance yet.'

As with many aspects of the solo life, it can take time to get things just right. Clearly to be nomadic you need to have a few things around you to be assured of success.

Most crucial is obviously having access to the tools of your trade. So if your laptop is one of the key components of your mobile business, do you have a good, reliable backup? Do you have enough battery life? What would happen if your laptop was lost or stolen?

All of these factors need to be carefully thought through because if something can go wrong, at some point it probably will. What are your insurance policies like? What if you lose access to your files and data for an extended period? How would you handle that?

For pretty well every eventuality, there are solutions; it's just a matter of anticipating these things, planning out what might happen.

If you're going to be a mobile soloist, particularly one who hops between time zones, you'll need to let your clients know what to expect when it comes to contact and response times. You'll need to establish how and when you'll interact and communicate.

Keeping clients at bay

In case you've not noticed already, establishing guidelines and boundaries with clients is an essential ingredient of a happy solo life, regardless of where you're working.

In the early years of my consulting and coaching business when my son was very young, while I wasn't particularly nomadic, I did move around a fair bit invariably pounding the pavements with a pram. In such instances it was important to me that I didn't take phone calls. To balance my need for control while maintaining a strong sense of accessibility I established guidelines with my clients whereby contact with me was only via email. I had a dual-sim mobile phone and simply let all work-related calls go through to voicemail outside of my chosen work hours.

I set up this understanding with clients from the start with a 'how we'll work together' document that I provided for them at the start of a new relationship. One agreement was that I would be the one who would initiate any phone conversation, but I did also make a pledge that I would be super responsive to any messages.

So if a client wanted me, I positioned myself as available, but with me controlling the nature and time of dialogue. Clients like to know what they can expect from you and in my experience will always respect boundaries once they see that you do.

There are stacks of benefits of being mobile. It can be quite a cost saving. I know plenty of soloists who simply don't need a 'proper office'. They save money on leases, office fit-outs, electricity, internet and so on, and with all essential business tools online these days – accounting, communications, collaboration, marketing – there's really no need to compromise on productivity.

Indeed, working remotely can have a positive impact on productivity as you're forced to organise yourself more and this in turn gives you increased focus in the hours you spend working.

By moving around you'll increase your horizons and view of the world, resulting in fresh ideas and strategies.

One of the key benefits newbie soloists talk about when first going it alone is the explosion of ideas and the inspiration that follows as a consequence of working 'outside the cubicle'.

Very rarely do we get our best ideas at our desk, staring at our monitor!

LOCATION, LOCATION, LOCATION

Without getting too carried away, jot down three places where you think you'd enjoy working:

1.
2.
3.

Define Your Work Style

Establish structures that work

While many soloists, notably those from the creative-services sector, claim to thrive on a lack of structure, most individuals really need it. You'll be amazed by the creative freedom you get from structure.

If you're running your solo business alongside other commitments, such as looking after children, then your productive time can be like gold; structure is essential to help you squeeze the most out of your time at work.

Let's look at where to start.

Firstly you'll need to consider your own strengths to develop your own unique work style. The key is to identify the times you feel most energised and focused, and structure your work time accordingly.

You may be most productive and energetic early in the mornings. That's definitely not me, by the way, but one of my colleagues starts at an absurd, unfathomable 4am!

What needs to happen, and what conditions do you need, to be your most productive self? Let's delve a little deeper and hopefully your ideal pattern will emerge.

Secure your boundaries

One problem I see time and again is poor boundaries.

Soloists are very susceptible to self-distraction, with constant checking of email and social media the biggest culprits.

But we also face an additional layer of interruptions and distractions. It's all too easy for our friends, our family and our neighbours to wrongly assume that because we work for ourselves we are always available to them for a chat or a visit.

You'd never hear this at the front door of an investment bank:

'Yoo-hoo, anybody home? I was in the area and thought I'd pop in for a quick cuppa!'

Sure, it can be great when an old friend or family member drops in unannounced, but not when it's 2.30pm on a Thursday and you've got a major project due at 5pm.

Not to mention the endless stream of 'quick' jobs that can rapidly eat into your work day, whether it's briefing the electrician, rescuing the washing before it rains, or picking up a sick child from school.

If you don't set clear boundaries, you can lose hours each day and seriously damage the viability of your business.

People around you need to know what's okay and you need to guide them, making it crystal clear when it's okay to interrupt you and when they should leave you alone.

With very young children, this is easier said than done, as social media adviser Nigel Emerson told me. Here he shares how his young daughter would wander into his office and want to chatter and generally get his undivided attention.

'In the early days I tried to distract her while I continued to write that very important letter, or finish the project I was working on. Then I would feel guilty that I was wasting our precious time together on work stuff when I could be engrossed with her.

'So I learned how to "swap hats" in an instant. From solopreneur to dad in three seconds flat. And I learned how to go back from dad to independent professional in the same amount of time.'

Children and family aside, we can do a lot to set up systems that minimise interruptions.

For example, many of us can make better use of voicemail and autoresponders. Changing the voicemail on your phone takes a few seconds and yet so few of us ever utilise this feature.

It's very easy to change a message to say:

'Hey, it's Tuesday afternoon at one o'clock. I've just got my head down on some client work. I will be available again at five o'clock. Leave a message and I'll call you back then.'

Of course you can switch your phone to silent while completing blocks of work, but I favour turning it off altogether. More generally I'd also suggest going through your phone and doing a 'notification audit'. Is it really necessary for you to receive alerts? And what are they costing you in terms of interruption and distraction?

Respect and value your time

When we recognise and display the value of our work time, it reassures us of our own efficiency and sends a strong message to friends, family, clients and customers. They are left in no doubt that they're dealing with someone who is focused, dedicated and serious. If we respect our time, they will too.

I recently attempted to lure a well-established and very successful entrepreneur onto my podcast show as I wanted to interview him. I wasn't convinced I'd succeed and I didn't. He let me down gently with these well-chosen words:

> *'Sorry, Robert, I've a lot on the go currently and the scale of the opportunity you're offering isn't quite there for me to shift my focus. Can you contact me again in a couple of months?'*

I immediately knew where I stood and admired his clarity of direction.

Ideally you'd set up a tight structure and approach in your solo venture from day one, but more realistically it is something that evolves over time and needs continual adjustments as you go.

CREATE A FORCE FIELD

What are three clear boundaries that may dramatically improve your work effectiveness?

1.

2.

3.

Plan your ideal week

One of the biggest benefits of going solo is freedom of choice. How we live and work is entirely up to us. Yeehah!

We have two distinct choices:

- We can work on purpose and follow a plan and structure of our own design.
- We can take things as they come, responding to the moods and demands of everyone else.

'If you don't design your own life plan, chances are you'll fall into someone else's plan. And guess what they have planned for you? Not much.'

I tend to agree with these words from author and entrepreneur Jim Rohn.

So what is it to be for you: proactive or reactive?

While we can't control every hour of the day – in business as in life, there will be surprises along the way – we can only accomplish what matters most when we confidently become the leader of our own life, and begin with the end in mind.

One of the ways to do this is by creating 'your ideal week'. Think of it as a budget for your time. Instead of working out how to spend your money, you're figuring out how best to spend your time.

I've long favoured the concept of blocks of time; that's to say a period whether a few short minutes or a longer chunk of a couple of hours, even an entire day, dedicated to one single, focused activity.

In the early days of my consulting business, one such block for me was Wednesday. Wednesdays were my 'business-development days'.

For a good few months, every action on a Wednesday had to do with marketing and business development. Anything and everything else simply had to wait. Interestingly, my Wednesdays were always full, as my mind was on the lookout for activities during the rest of the week. 'What's happening on Wednesday?' was the constant question coming from my subconscious.

Allocating that day also allowed me to shelve any thoughts on the topic I'd have at other times in the week, simply noting them and knowing that I'd get to it on Wednesday.

Louise Tomlinson, a freelance chef, uses a similar technique to keep her admin under control:

'I've been trialling a slightly different method of scheduling everything, involving the allocation of two hours for admin.

'If I don't have two hours of admin a day, then I get to work on one of my recipes. This stops me from squandering my time

replying to emails, quoting, invoicing and so on, as my kitchen time is my fun time!'

These days, I no longer have full-day blocks, but instead have solid periods blocked out for specific activities, not unlike Louise, and mine are not all work-related either.

I walk for an hour every day; I do yoga twice a week; I write for regular two-hour periods; I research new podcast guests, and all these are articulated in my ideal week.

In my diary I plan for the week I'd ideally like to live and work. By necessity, mine has a fair few component parts and is quite detailed, but white space is scheduled too so it's not end-to-end activity. And yes, there's always room for surprises.

I know for sure that without a picture and a plan, time becomes disjointed and unproductive. Personally that leaves me feeling noticeably unfulfilled at the end of the week, and more susceptible to stress and worry.

This ideal week process doesn't need to be complex. You can map it out in a simple grid or online calendar. Or, like me, simply use a page-per-day diary.

You may like to give individual days a theme. While I had business-development Wednesday, my Friday afternoons were known, to me anyway, as my 'do what the hell I want' block.

For this structure to be useful, it's vital to lock in activities that are important for your health and wellbeing and relationships, not just your work. Get all these things into your diary first.

Commonly when out giving talks and presentations, I meet burnt-out soloists lamenting all the activities they'd sacrificed for their business: going for a walk, playing soccer with their mates; taking their partner out for a regular dinner; visiting art galleries or going to the movies.

These were the very activities that gave them the energy they needed to start their businesses in the first place!

Such activities rejuvenate and re-energise us. As soloists, we owe it to ourselves and our business to build them into our ideal week and not let them fall by the wayside when we're busy.

Good weeks make for good months that turn into good years. Your ideal week is an essential building block of a life well lived.

DIARY DATES

What activities would you like to see in your diary? Keep a note of some favourites.

5.

Map Your Path

Work out where you're going

'The world steps aside for the man who knows where he is going.'

Fine words from James Allen, grandfather of the motivational movement and author of the 1902 classic, *As a Man Thinketh*.

We soloists would do well to take Allen's words to heart. It comes down to having an inspired picture of where your solo business is headed. The best way to get that picture is to start work on a vision.

A vision is a mental projection of your future and the reason you really need one is it clarifies precisely where you want your solo adventure to take you. What's more, the instant you express a vision, your goals are given some substance.

A vision is different from a mission. A vision is a picture of where you are headed, whereas a mission states a broader purpose. For example, a person whose vision says, 'I will become a qualified physiotherapist' might have as a mission, 'I want to contribute to the alleviation of human suffering.'

Before we delve further, let me share this little gem from my good friend Deborah Kneeshaw. A while ago we were down at the beach together talking about the power of holding a vision, and she told me how it helped her get the courage to take up ocean swimming.

'I'd always been uncertain about my ability to swim in the ocean. While I found the water beyond the breaking waves really appealing, I was unsure how to make my way there through the waves.

'I knew I needed to start seeing it, if I was ever going to achieve it!

'Before I even set foot in the water, though, for three after-noons, I watched the waves for an hour until I understood how, why and when the wave patterns were formed. I also used this time to talk to ocean swimmers before and after their swim. They were happy to pass on tips about how to deal with the breakers. I made mental notes as I watched how they entered and left the surf and little by little I envisaged myself doing the same.

'On the fourth day, the water was relatively calm and I knew it was time to dip my toe in. Before long I ventured out on a short swim. By Friday I had enough confidence to tackle the surf. But before I went in the water, I walked out onto the rocks beyond the waves to remind myself just how beautiful the still waters really were.

'Back on the beach I picked my moment, waiting till after a big set had come through to leap in. Soon I was swimming through the waves, moving through the water using a strong, rhythmic stroke. Before I knew it I was safely beyond the surf and immersed in balmy turquoise waters. I'd made it!'

And that's precisely what a vision does: it gives you the confidence and belief that you can do this.

Let's back all this up with some hard facts.

Research undertaken by Hal Hershfield, then an assistant professor in the marketing department of New York University's Stern School of Business, and Kelly McGonigal, a health psychologist and lecturer at Stanford University, showed that when people realistically imagined their future selves in a clear and considered way, they were motivated to make choices and decisions to benefit that future self.

This stands to reason when you think about it. When we can see a picture of our future, we're far more likely to be drawn and energised by the path that leads towards it. Just as Deborah did by picturing herself in the calm blue ocean.

A well-articulated vision gives you a full picture of your ideal business *and* life. It should take you out of your comfort zone, but not into the twilight zone. While being ambitious is encouraged, being unrealistic is not.

I really like this Japanese proverb:

'Vision without action is a daydream. Action without vision is a nightmare.'

Essentially, a vision enables the creation of a unique personal manifesto that can be used to direct your actions and determine the decisions you make. It's a combination of your motivations (i.e. what you want), your values (what you believe) and your abilities (what you have to offer).

Your vision will ensure you are exactly where you need to be, in the driver's seat and heading in the right direction.

Visions have the power to not only guide you to your dream destination, but to act as a magnet drawing you towards it. No wonder these are such a powerful weapon in the soloist's arsenal!

If you doubt whether you've ever experienced the power of a vision as Hershfield and McGonigal indicated, I'll bet you have.

You know when you're planning to go off on a much-needed holiday and you start to imagine what it'll be like when you get there?

You can already picture yourself lying on the beach. You can almost hear the waves breaking on the shore, feel the balmy coastal breeze, the sun warming your skin and the sand between your toes. A smile breaks out on your face and you start to unwind. This is you envisioning your holiday. You're nowhere near your destination and yet you've effectively transported yourself there.

By doing the same thing in your business, you can help draw yourself towards where you want to be.

The best visions aren't set in stone; instead they're living, breathing things that remain open to your questions and challenges and can be adapted accordingly.

I'll finish with another fascinating finding from researchers at UCLA who wanted to know why the Chinese population were much less likely to suffer obesity, far less likely to smoke and 30 per cent more likely to save for retirement than their US counterparts.

Quite remarkably, they concluded it had to do with how readily this nation could envisage their future selves and therefore what a relatively 'easy sell' it was to take greater care now.

And the main explanation was language.

In English, the speaker is forced to consider correct grammar and tense in relation to verbs and sentence construction. For example, it rained, it's raining, it will rain. But in Mandarin, the construction is much simpler: yesterday rain, today rain, tomorrow rain.

The researchers found this nuance of language enables the people of China – in the case of saving for retirement, for example – to fully associate and respond *today* to something that many in other countries fail to take seriously until much later in life. And often too late.

In the same way, a clear vision gives you the same sense of ongoing surety by providing a seamless, inspired and inspiring path.

REMEMBER WHEN?

We'll be coming to some vision exercises shortly; for now though, just note a couple of memories where holding a vision (no matter how slight or vague) helped you.

For me, it was moving to the big city, London, in my twenties. I simply couldn't stop seeing it. As the picture grew in detail, the move became inevitable.

What to do when the path is not clear

Whether you run an established business, or dream of going it alone, the picture of the future is rarely crystal clear. There will be gaps and confusion about where to next and how. That was certainly the case for me.

In the early 1990s, having spent twenty years in London, I relocated from one side of the globe to the other in moving from London to Sydney.

Arriving in Australia, fresh from a career in marketing and design and with a couple of minor sideline soloist forays, I had at best a blurry picture of my future.

A vision had got me to Sydney. But now what?

I knew I wanted to use my skills and interests in some way, and create an ideal lifestyle led by my business. It's fair to say I arrived in my new location somewhat weary and burnt out, and I knew from that point that in my next venture, I would need to focus more keenly on my mental and physical wellbeing.

My vision had massive gaps, but a few things were very clear. I knew the kind of people I wanted to surround myself with (other lifestyle-conscious people). I knew where I wanted to live; right down to the look, feel and airiness of the rooms, the furniture, the colours and fragrances, and I definitely had a clear image of the workspace I wanted.

But what I had little idea about was what I'd actually do – my actual vocation – and therefore how I'd earn any income. That's quite a gap!

This situation may be familiar to some of you right now and it can be quite concerning and debilitating. I get that, but don't worry if your picture is fuzzy to start with. We all have to begin somewhere. It's the *start* that's important.

> ## MIND THE GAP
>
> A good way to start defining your vocational sweet spot is to jot down all the answers you can think of to these questions:
> 1. What do you love?
> 2. What are you good at?
> 3. What does the world need?
> 4. What can you be paid for?
>
> At the point where these answers start to intersect, you'll find the pieces of a new career and business opportunities that align with the other elements of your vision.
>
> It may all feel a bit like a jigsaw. Trust me when I say the pieces will all come together. Just have patience!

Surprising benefits of a vision

Once you have started forming your own inspiring vision, the most exciting part is actually putting it into action. When yours starts working its magic, you'll wonder how you ever functioned without one.

While visions can be perceived as intangible, in fact they can be put to use in your business in all manner of practical ways. Here are my top five benefits.

1. You find decision-making a breeze

As you move along the soloist path, you'll inevitably encounter tempting forks in the road that branch off all over the place.

With no vision guiding your choice, you pick a path arbitrarily and wander off, never really getting closer to a goal or knowing where you'll end up.

With a vision, you have an oracle to consult whenever you need to decide which track to take. Before making a choice you can ask yourself: 'Does collaborating with this person/moving to this location/accepting this assignment fit with my vision?'

If yes, proceed with confidence; if no, hit delete.

2. You stay focused

In the early days of a new business it's easy to be attracted by the bright lights of new opportunities. A vision keeps you focused on your priorities. Acting with such focus and purpose, even in the face of adversity, means you can't help but make progress. To paraphrase James Allen, the world steps aside for soloists who know where they're going.

3. You become so productive

Every time you wonder aloud 'Why am I doing this?' your vision provides the answer. It helps you see the method in your madness and is therefore a potent driving force, giving you the energy needed to clear any obstacles blocking your path. If you've been running your business for years, your vision reminds you with a jolt just why you started the adventure.

Even boring chores become imbued with a sense of purpose, making them a lot easier to execute than if your prime motivation is just a sense of obligation.

4. You attract opportunities

Your enthusiasm and obvious sense of purpose has a stunning effect on your sphere of influence. If your vision truly inspires you, others will find it infectious and new opportunities will come your way as people, captivated by your clarity and vitality, will likely want to be associated with you. In effect you create your own personal cheer squad of supporters.

If you know where you're headed and you articulate that through your work, others will be drawn to you.

Ponder for a moment someone whom you consider to be clear, together and focused. Like to get to know them better? Fancy working with them? Thought so.

5. You're never short of inspiration

A meaningful vision can be your very own portable coach, acknowledging, challenging and supporting you as you move forward.

In fact your vision is the best motivational tool you'll find.

A LETTER FROM THE FUTURE

For this exercise sit yourself down somewhere nice. A place where you feel calm, comfortable and creative. For many this is not the office, but might be another area of the house, at a public library, in a café, park or at the beach.

Turn off your phone, clear your mind and write me a letter. Yes, really.

But here's the thing: this letter is from the future. One year from now. It's a letter that describes your view of the ideal world. It's not where you are now; it's where you want to be.

In your letter, tell me what you're up to. How your business looks. Where you're spending your time. I'd like to know about stuff outside work as well – friendships, relationships, your outlook on life and your health.

Name names; be specific; get it all down. Take your time and keep it real. You may even like to have a close friend, partner or family member undertake the same exercise.

When it's finished, send it to me c/o your own address. When you receive the letter, I give you permission to open it, read it carefully and circle the major advances from your current situation in red pen. These will become your goals for the year ahead, the areas of life and work that demand your attention.

Just try it; you may be surprised by the new goals and orientation that emerge from this exercise.

The power of pictures

But wait, there's more! More ways to bring your vision to life.

I was first introduced to the process of creating a 'vision board' at a small workshop many years ago and my original creation still resides in my home office.

I'd recently met Jane, who is now my wife, and was working full-time in my consulting and coaching business. I had the germ of an idea to do something different, something bigger, but at the time was very hazy about what that may be.

The vision-board exercise involves tearing out images from magazines that have some kind of personal significance when thinking of an exciting and inspiring future, and then pasting them onto a nice sizeable board.

The images combine to depict a picture of the future.

Some of the images depicted my personal life – in my case some glossy magazine pictures of airy, arty homes; a picture of a contented and relaxed partner (seeing Jane relaxed happens to be one of my key measures of success); and, shock-horror, an image of a child (we had no definite plans at that stage!).

And of course, there were images that illustrated my work – my dream colleagues, my ideal workspace, and an indication of the impact I wanted this mythical business to have on the world at large.

Looking at my vision board now never ceases to amaze me, as *everything* I depicted has come to pass.

A blog post I wrote on the topic of vision boards generated a stack of great comments from fellow soloists, including these:

'Love my vision board. I use a cork noticeboard that hangs right in front of me every day, just above my computer screen. I also have some heart-shaped stickers on hand that I stick all over images of things as they are realised.'

'I have many amazing examples of things that have materialised, right down to sentences I imagined clients and other significant players saying!'

And this from Jayne Tancred, who ended up joining our little team:

'My vision board had me working with some really cool folk who love helping small-business owners achieve great things and have fun doing it!'

SCISSORS AND GLUE

Grab yourself a nice big sheet of board and some old magazines, and get to work creating your own vision board. I reckon you too will be pleasantly surprised by the power that comes from a collection of inspiring images.

6.

Be the Best You

You have what it takes

Dan Pink has written a score of bestsellers including *Drive: The Surprising Truth About What Motivates Us*. You may have seen his accompanying TED talk on the puzzle of motivation. It's one of the most watched TED talks of all time.

Dan is someone I've admired and stalked for years, and not just because he gave my first book a rather wonderful testimonial.

In one of his early books, *Free Agent Nation,* Dan made it crystal clear he gets soloism, but it's in the more recent *Drive* that he's penned a book that could have been written especially for us.

In it he distils and comments on a variety of international research programs that have looked at what makes people do what they do most effectively and happily, whether in life or work.

He concluded, backed by data from behavioural scientists and psychologists, that our motivational drive comes from three key factors: autonomy, mastery and purpose. I believe soloism offers each in abundance.

Autonomy

Autonomy essentially means having control over what you do and how you do it – managing your time, making decisions on the services you provide and for whom. There can be few things other than soloism that will bring you true autonomy!

Mastery

The next is mastery – being able to use and improve your skills. While mastery is attainable outside of soloism, surely very few workplaces accommodate such freedom to learn and grow when and how you choose.

Purpose

And finally, purpose – making a difference and doing work that has meaning. Work that has value for you and the world at large.

I invite you to watch Dan's TED talk, as I feel sure you too will recognise the ability of soloism to provide all these elements of drive.

Soloism is a way of working where it's not only your right to be yourself; it's your duty.

'To business that we love we rise betime. And go to't with delight.'

Judging by that quote, William Shakespeare grasped the concept and those who get the most out of soloism know that being themselves is not just good for the soul, it's also very good for business.

Soloists who turn up 100 per cent love their work and it loves them right back.

Self-awareness – 'knowing yourself', your values and what drives you – gives you the confidence to *be* yourself.

Ultimately if, when you hold a mirror up to yourself, you don't truly understand who you are and what motivates you, your words and actions will not be cohesive or in harmony, and your business will suffer.

Living and working with authenticity boosts your confidence and leads to contentment.

A few years ago, I asked a roomful of new and established soloists, varying in age from their early thirties to over sixty, what it was about working for themselves that they enjoyed so much. Here are some of their comments:

'I no longer have to unwind. The pace of my business is the pace of my life.'

'I'm happy to bump into work contacts, even on the weekends.'

'I seem to attract people who have similar values to my own.'

'I feel an overriding sense of freedom each and every day.'

'I thought I hated marketing and yet I can talk readily about what I do without boring the life out of people.'

'I say what I need to say and do what I need to do without struggling with what I ought to say or ought to do.'

Wonderful sentiments, wouldn't you say? Let's do a little exercise to reinforce this whole notion of how the approach we take to our work impacts the prosperity of our venture.

THE TALE OF TWO CAFÉS

Pause for a few moments and consider two mythical cafés, both making decent coffee. One is bustling and successful, the other much less so. One is loved by the owner, the other is not. Perhaps real-life cafés spring to mind. They do for me!

So with the image of each in your mind, scribble some words or doodle emoticons alongside these questions:

The customer perspective	Loved café	Unloved café
1. What's the overall ambience like, and how does it feel to be there?		
2. How pleasant is the lighting and décor?		
3. Think about cleanliness. Crisp or shabby? (And don't forget to check the bathrooms.)		
4. Let's look at the staff. Warm, friendly and helpful, or harried and inconsiderate?		
5. If the owner is evident, what kind of vibe are you getting? Smiley or grumpy?		

I'm guessing that wasn't too much of a challenge. It's easy to see that how we show up and behave in our business can really impact the success of our solo venture. In the same way you wouldn't work with a time-management consultant who's late for meetings or a fashion designer who's an unco-ordinated mess, you too need to be 100 per cent aligned with your business if you are to attract your ideal clients.

Handling rejection and staying upbeat

Whether it's in the throes of setting up your business, a little way down the track, or even after you've been doing what you do for ages, I promise you, someday, someone is going to give you a healthy dose, or potentially unhealthy dose, of rejection.

For some it's a regular occurrence. Take, for example, those soloists who out of necessity are regularly cold calling, whether to sell products or services or to make appointments.

The first thing to realise is that regardless of what you do, it won't be for everyone. Some people will love your product or services, some people won't. What's needed is to focus atten-tion on the people that do support what you do, and ensure there are enough of them to sustain your business.

Anyone putting out any kind of work into the world faces criticism.

'If people like what I do, fantastic. If they don't, that's good too.'

That's from Ricky Gervais, creator of classic mockumentary *The Office*. In his interview with the *Harvard Business Review*, he went on to say that if you start trying to dilute or pander too much to your audience, you end up with something so safe and homogenised that while a few like it, they won't love it.

Not everyone loves Ricky Gervais, but those who do love most of everything he does and with a passion.

Ideally we'll have done enough research to ensure that when we give *our* sales pitch, it's to people who are interested in hearing it.

But when it comes to coping with the cold shoulder, we can take a good lesson from those in what's known as the 'high-rejection' business.

Namely, the cold callers and telemarketers. They will tell you that for all the rejections, there's also the occasional yes. But if you're not out there actually getting those nos, then the yeses aren't going to come either.

At certain stages in your business, you'll need to be spreading your marketing messages; 'selling', in other words. By remembering that it's a numbers game and a yes will *always* require a few nos, we can embrace rejection as just part of the journey.

Don't take rejection personally. While that's easy to say, it can be hard to keep in mind, especially when you are passionate about what you do. People aren't rejecting you, even if they're not buying what you're offering. They're just saying they're not after what you have to offer right now.

Even in the face of rejection or criticism, you can remain polite, pass on some helpful information and acknowledge feedback.

It could so happen the people saying no now may need your services down the track. If you're supportive and responsive, they'll remember you.

Finally, if you can avoid being defensive, there's lots to learn from rejection. Once you give it some thought, it might be that your approach could be improved, your pitch sharpened or even your offering adapted.

So when you get a rejection, do pause for a second and just make sure that you've taken all the lessons that there are to be had before getting back on the horse!

It's a myth that the customer is always right! But they're not always wrong either.

Making a first impression without being there

For the purposes of this topic, let's assume I've come across you while searching online as I'm interested in the kind of stuff you provide.

Even though we haven't met, that doesn't mean I can't form an opinion about you.

Good old word-of-mouth has long been the strongest source of new business for soloists. But once you move beyond this one-to-one sphere, your reputation essentially boils down to what people can dig up about you online.

As a soloist, your website may be the closest thing you have to a traditional CV or resumé, but everything posted online will be fair game for scrutiny. And like most, your website will attribute significantly more weight and credibility to what other people say about you than what you say about yourself. Content such as testimonials, ratings, reviews, case studies and the rest all tell a valuable story.

This notion, referred to as *personal branding* or *reputation management*, can mean different things to different people.

On balance I think Jeff Bezos, founder of Amazon, sums it up perfectly when he says that branding is what other people say about you when you're not in the room. Very apt for the concept of personal branding.

Whether you love the idea or hate it, the reality is that you probably already have a personal brand online and it's either working for you or against you.

Give me your name, business name and a few minutes on Google and I'll form an opinion, good or bad, right or wrong, informed, uninformed or misinformed.

This profile is already out there as a blurry digital footprint, so you need to be aware of what comes up.

Go on, google yourself! And when you're doing this, don't just search your name; also look up any email addresses you have or have had and any phone numbers you own. You'll be surprised how often these too throw up some kind of personal history.

Be conscious of how your various social media profiles may come across to curious potential clients. If this worries you, consider adjusting your privacy settings.

With luck, if you come up at all, you'll come up well – but be sure to dig down a little way. Visit the eerily quiet Google results on pages three, four and five just to be sure.

Google's findings for you may be a bit dodgy; not necessarily bad, just not terribly good. While it's not easy to remove the old stuff that appears on search engines, what you can do is dominate Google with plenty of the new stuff.

Make sure that any editable profiles that exist for you online,

LinkedIn being a key example, project what you want them to project and lead with *today's* you, not some past, slightly outmoded and irrelevant you. It's hard to pass as a leading professional if all a prospect sees is tired and dusty.

What you want people to see is what you want to be known for. It's time to start building those kind of search results now.

Alongside what people see when they search for you, you'll need to consider the impression you give when you appear in their inbox, their social feeds or indeed alongside them at a networking function.

Fluffymouse74@hotmail.com isn't going to be doing you any favours. A badly cropped wedding photo won't cut it as your profile picture. As well as updating your written profile, consider getting a professional headshot done – it can be used everywhere and is worth its weight in gold.

Prospects will be more willing to invest in you if you look like you've invested in yourself. And how seriously you're taken is directly related to how seriously you take yourself.

You'll never know when opportunity might be knocking (or googling!) so make sure you've got your best foot forward.

GOOGLE YOURSELF!

See what comes up for your name, your business name and your email address. Now imagine a prospective customer is standing behind you. Does anything need changing?

Have you painted your Ferrari?

While we should never judge a book by its cover, we must also face the reality that people do!

Soloists face a crowded marketplace. Your customers have lots of choice and many of your competitors will present themselves and their businesses with a sharp, bright and polished sheen.

When you're competing in this kind of arena, good enough isn't good enough. You have to get attention, and one way is to be visually professional, powerful and memorable.

Today's successful soloists don't have grubby business cards, ill-conceived logos or noisy, nasty, cluttered websites – and neither should you.

There are thousands of good books, articles and videos explaining the basics and importance of branding and positioning, so take some time to understand how you wish your brand to be presented.

We don't want to see a chopped-off, blurry photo on your About page. We don't want typos or slapdash designs, and, sorry, but we're not too bothered about your long, boring resumé. You're going solo.

I'm being harsh, but my point is that seemingly superficial things like product branding, packaging, emotional connection, glossy design and nice writing are absolutely integral to the quality and success of your key product, YOU.

There are lots of brilliant people and technically superior products that never truly capture a market's imagination, let alone its wallet.

You may have done all the hard work to gain your skills or

create a product, but if you fail to invest in the all-important polish, it lessens the value in the eye of customers.

It's like designing and constructing a super-exotic, super-expensive Ferrari, and then not worrying about the paint job.

Here's what my marketing buddy Tim Reid said in a blog post to the Flying Solo community:

> 'Do things properly. If this means doing less, then do less. Avoid cheap, shoddy anything: printing, design, packaging, photography and copy.'

And I reckon he's spot on. Your prospects want you clean, clear, uncluttered and professional. If you try to do everything on the cheap, you risk compromising your success, and cheap may well be all you'll ever be able to afford.

Give us the best you can. One page done beautifully trumps a mass of mediocrity.

Put yourself first

The topics of health, wellbeing, exercise and nutrition are all subjects covered in a plethora of individual books, TV shows and documentaries, so rather than attempt to deep dive into those areas, let me instead give you some basics relevant to running a solo business. And if I touch a nerve, well, perhaps that signals that something needs your attention!

As a soloist on a journey to create a business you can love, you'll need to show up for work in the best possible shape you can.

If you are stressed about things, you won't sleep well. If you don't sleep well, you won't operate well and if you don't operate well, you'll get more stressed.

But you know this stuff, right?

Diet and exercise impacts how you work and how you feel. A big night out will likely impede the start of a new day. If you're undernourished or dehydrated, eat a banana or drink some water! And if you think a long stodgy lunch will help your energy, best think again!

Exercise not only boosts your energy and improves your health, it'll open up the pathways in your mind that lead to innovative new ideas.

It amuses me that so many of us talk about not having enough hours in the day, when what we're really saying is we don't have sufficient energy to make the most of the time we have.

This comment from voiceover artist Virginia Muzon shows she's made the connection between time and energy management:

'I'm allowing myself more time each day for things like medi-tation and breaks to foster more energy. And having two dogs means I get out for that daily dose of nature too.'

I've spoken with hundreds of groups of soloists over the past decade or so and often ask them, 'When do you have your best ideas?' No-one ever responded by saying they have their best ideas when they're in their office staring at their screen.

The prosperity of a solo business demands an approach that constantly brims with innovation and new ideas, and for this we need to get into the habit of moving away from our desk. Getting out and getting active is one of the best ways to do this.

Researchers from Stanford examined creativity levels of people while they walked versus while they sat.

Quite amazingly, a person's creative output increased by an average of 60 per cent when walking. Sixty per cent!

But wait, there's more. And this is encouraging, even for those who don't like walking. A study from the University of Notre Dame found that the mere action of stepping through a doorway can reset the brain and it's been suggested this is why we can forget what we are looking for when we enter a new room.

So getting up and moving away from your desk is a great way to get your brain to 'start fresh' and come at something from a different direction.

A little tip to aid mental energy

Let's not forget that energy is greatly influenced not just by what we eat and drink, but also by how we think and feel, and, importantly, by those around us.

An old mate of mine, a somewhat jaded ad man, let's call him 'Stephen', became so sick of dealing with unreasonable people he invented a new rule. Here's what he told me, in his own frank words:

> 'From today I have "The No A***hole Rule". I'm simply going to refuse to do any work for anyone I don't like. Life's too short to try to please energy-sappers.'

Okay, well that's nice and clear! How is that new rule working for him? Not too badly, as it turns out. Far from turning him into an increasingly cranky soloist, it's making him set the bar higher. He asks better questions, he listens more deeply and by demanding more of his potential customers it seems he's giving more of himself.

Mindfulness

I can't end this section without at least touching on mindfulness and meditation. If you've not felt the benefit of being present – that is, in the now, not the past or the future – then this is the time to learn about it and practise it.

WHAT GETS YOUR CREATIVE JUICES FLOWING?

Let's look at how and when you generate your best ideas. Write down three clear situations that spring to mind:

1.

2.

3.

7.

Seize Your Market

Who gives a damn?

You may not know this. I'll be surprised if you do. The Francois Langur monkey, a native of South-East Asia, is born tiny and bright orange, a total contrast to its large, dark parents.

Neither ethnologists nor anthropologists can fully agree why this is. But the most compelling reason so far is that Francois Langur monkeys are more attracted to fresh fruit than they are to newborns. And so, the young get the attention of their parents by masquerading as oranges and mangoes. Isn't nature wondrous?

In your solo business, you have to know whose attention you're after. Who gives a damn about what you do?

You don't have to wear an orange suit or do anything drastic, just be crystal clear on who you're looking to attract.

I saw a presentation recently where a young travel guide excitedly spoke about specialising in *everything*. You want a retirees tour; you want a trip for your young family; you want to walk; you want to travel by bicycle: I'm your guide. Er, except you're not.

Like most, in today's crowded and noisy marketplace, I seek out specialists who can demonstrate that they really understand what I want and need.

Broad messages rarely get heard; that is, *truly* heard and listened to. They're more likely to disappear into the void of the marketplace. To succeed in soloism is to connect deeply with your audience. To do that well, you must inspire reactions like, 'She's talking to me.' 'He understands me.' 'She cares about my challenges.' 'I give a damn.'

Alice Hunt, a workwear distributor, remarked in one of our community forum discussions:

'I really thought my customer was everyone. This is so wrong.'

So wrong indeed. It's way better to be heard clearly by a few people than ignored by a hundred. The way to do this is to truly understand your product, and determine who is going to benefit most from it and how.

Then shape your messages to appeal to that specific audience.

Making sure there's a market

CB Insights in New York ran some research that looked at over 100 start-up ventures that hadn't worked out. They'd flopped.

The startling finding was that even though the typical

WHO'S IN THE ROOM?

Imagine a roomful of people who are the perfect customers for your business. They're in a nice comfortable setting, waiting for you to join them. No hard selling, no challenging questions. A lovely group of people.

Use the space below to note some of their characteristics. Don't think too hard, don't go into detail, just capture some evocative words.

'failure' had already raised significant investor finance – the average being $1.3m – they'd still bombed. And the main reason? No market need.

Forty-two per cent of businesses were focused on building a solution that was looking for a problem, rather than knowing the problem and designing the business to answer the need. Sounds like a fairly basic stuff-up, doesn't it? And yet it's easy to get all revved up with passion and excitement, listening to acclaim from friends and family, and forget to gauge 'real-world' demand.

At this point I must tell you that I have never bought into the whole 'nine out of ten small businesses fail' or eight out of ten or whatever statistic the scaremongers are peddling today. It's rubbish.

Most small businesses don't fail, and statistics and research bear this out. Undeniably a good number don't go as planned, some just get too hard and some soloists chuck the towel in early and return to the safety of employment. But spectacular, costly failure is rare. And it would be rarer still if all soloists spent more time researching the market.

Jane Taylor runs a herbal-essences business and is no stranger to seeking feedback on her plans and ideas:

> *'People like to be asked for their opinions, are extraordinarily generous with their time and relish the sense of contribution that comes from helping others succeed.'*

So let's look at some simple, practical ways to gauge the likelihood of a sufficient market existing for your new product, service or business idea.

Check out your competitors

Firstly, if you're smugly thinking you don't have any competitors, then you're starting to worry me! Very few businesses are unique. And when this claim is made, it's usually because the idea is not viable, not because it's the next Facebook. Ouch!

It's usually far better to take what others are doing and deliver it better or differently, than try to educate an entire population that they need something they've never heard of.

Start by checking out your competitors. Look at their websites, visit their stores, call them up, email them and ask them questions. If you spend enough time, you'll start to get a picture of how busy they are and the activities they undertake. Look at their social networks and read their reviews and testimonials.

In over a decade of supporting a large community of soloists, it's never ceased to amaze me how much information others will share if you only ask.

Heather Smith is a management accountant and has built a strong reputation as a soloist generous with her time and expertise. This summarises her attitude towards her competitors:

'I am fortunate to keep in close contact with my competitors both locally and nationally. Without them, I wouldn't be able to offer and maintain the service I do.

'When weighing up cooperation versus competition, I treat my competitors as my peers. They are a technical resource, provide support during busy times and back-up for when I go on holiday.'

It's never too early to start building competitor relationships; in fact, the earlier the better.

Talk to potential customers
Don't be intimidated by talking to potential customers. Bear in mind that you might only need to speak to a handful of people to get some good insights. Perhaps set aside a few hours a day for a week and review your results after that.

Make sure you're prepared, and whether you're calling people up or even stopping them in the street, ensure you have a list of questions ready to ask, plus, of course, a pen and paper or voice recorder handy to make as many notes as you can during and after each conversation.

You can learn so much by having good, focused conversations with real people. A catch-up in a café with three or four

> ## RESEARCH, RESEARCH, RESEARCH
>
> There's so much information and data that's available on the internet, so dig deep. Every hour you spend understanding the potential and breadth of your market is an investment of time that will pay you back in spades.

individuals you've pegged as potential customers – perhaps where you buy the coffees and cakes – can elicit some truly valuable pointers to the likely appeal of your business.

Inviting and using feedback

When starting up, running or reinventing your solo venture, getting honest and open feedback on the validity of your ideas will be of huge benefit.

If people like what you're doing, they'll tell you. And in my experience they'll tell you very clearly and very positively. A word of warning though: if they don't like your product, service, idea or strategy, they'll also say that very openly. So you need to have courage.

The more you put into defining exactly what it is that you'd like feedback on, the better it's going to be for everybody. You'll get productive feedback that you can actually use, but be ready to accept negative feedback that may come your way.

If you're not braced, negative feedback can tip you into thinking your idea is doomed, whereas we should be brave enough to view all feedback as an opportunity to see what's between you and success.

Feedback is new information that's there to help you improve regardless of what that feedback may be, what it sounds like, what it looks like and what it feels like. Embrace feedback, accept it as positive regardless of what it is, and you're on the cusp of banning the thought of failure totally.

Clear, safe and specific

So how do you get genuine 'warts and all' feedback?

The first thing is to create a safe environment for those you're inviting to comment and for yourself.

If you've ever been asked for feedback only to find the format means you can't respond meaningfully, or you're not offered anonymity, or there's not enough room on the form to say what you want to say, you probably won't bother.

You can avoid this by being very specific on what it is that you would like reviewed and setting the context. Is it your idea? Is it your logo? Is it your website? Is it your customer proposition? Is it your unique selling point?

By establishing a clear context, one where people understand broadly what it is that you do and who for, you'll be creating a scenario in which due consideration can be given to how well you're satisfying these objectives.

There's little point asking for feedback on a business name without giving a sense of what the business will do, the image it seeks to project and the culture it aims to exhibit.

In a blog post, personal and executive coach Margot Aristide explained her approach to feedback questions with this restaurant diner example:

'If you ask them how the meal was, they say "fine". That's a long way from "incredible". To me, "fine" is not helpful feedback. All too often we take feedback at face value. It's easy, polite and useless.

'Instead of "How was the meal?" try "What three things could we have done differently to make this better?"'

Get the questions right and you'll learn from the answers.

Many solo start-ups make the mistake of talking just to friends and family. The danger there is that they tend to be extreme and far from objective. Some can be overly optimistic because they want you to be happy, or they don't want to hurt your feelings. Others can be unreasonably negative because they want to protect you from risks or even feel threatened by your ambitions.

By all means talk to friends and family, but don't stop there. Go out of your way to extract honest feedback; it really is the most helpful kind.

A good place to get fresh, candid feedback can be online, via forums like Flying Solo's or those of other social media sites. For example, I've seen plenty of people post a few versions of their logo and asking others to vote on a favourite.

Alternatively, consider forming your own little focus group with three or four contacts, again being clear on what specifically you want feedback on.

The thing to always bear in mind with research and feedback is that while you may not hear what you'd like to hear, it's probable you'll hear what you *need* to hear.

8.

Get Your Offering Right

Testing early-stage ideas

When it comes to assessing the need for your new service, product or business idea, I suggest you heed the Roman proverb 'forewarned is forearmed'!

An essential step in the development of your business is to validate the likely appeal of your product or service. Ideally this can be done way before you've invested too much time or money.

Think of it as a means of testing your assumptions. Do people actually want or need this product or service?

Fortunately there are straightforward tools that you can use to test and demonstrate the value of your business concepts and propositions, so let's look at a few.

For the purposes of this, I'm going to assume you have a

pretty strong idea of your offering and a good picture of your target market. So the exercise is to effectively put a toe in the water, or do some 'shadow testing' as they say at the big end of town.

Shadow testing is the process of actually selling or promoting an offering, often before it actually exists.

Regardless of whether your business is going to have a large online presence, tapping into the massive number of people who are online all day every day is the perfect way to gauge the response from a targeted audience.

Landing pages

A landing page is a basic, single-purpose web page where you can describe your product or service and test images, headlines, copy and offers. They are tailor-made for the soloist – just google 'landing pages' and you'll find a mass of low-cost or free services offering these.

With the simplest of landing pages, you can trial your messages and offer to see if it resonates with your target audience. For example, you might provide a downloadable report on the topic, or invite people to sign up for an early-bird offer as soon as the product launches.

Once your page is set up, you're going to need some visitors. Using the low-cost advertising options on platforms such as Google, Facebook, Twitter or LinkedIn can be a great way to reach a highly targeted audience.

You begin by picking your target market. If you want, you can get extremely granular, specifying precise ages, locations, interests and so on.

Next put a budget on how much you're prepared to spend

and very quickly the clicks and conversions from these ads will give you valuable insights on what appealed to people and why . . . or why not!

Google's keyword planner is a wonderful free and helpful service in this area that will help you select the relevant and related search terms. You'll find it useful both in crafting your ads and propositions, and seeing what the most popular terms are in your market.

Make phone calls!

Calling potential customers is another great way to get real insights quickly. Landing pages will certainly help quantify demand, but talking with prospects gives you a deeper understanding of *why* they want it.

Through these conversations you'll also identify the things you need to improve to have the greatest appeal to your market. But to get the best results, it's important to be respectful of people's time. People are understandably wary of cold calls, so perhaps you could invite some warm leads by canvassing friends or friends of friends, or reaching out for help via social media.

You could think about offering a discount or some kind of financial motivation to those helping you out in exchange for their time and feedback.

Sell it on eBay

If you're selling products and have a quantity ready to go, eBay is an efficient and fairly immediate way to see if people are willing to buy it and how much they'll pay.

eBay provide the traffic, handle the transaction process and have an online presence that is established and trusted, all of which can make it a fine place to test the popularity of your offering.

And even if you're thinking that eBay buyers are not your buyers, I suggest the process may be worthwhile as what you can learn covers a lot more than you may expect.

Architectural fittings retailer Nishad clearly needed convincing when he said this to me in conversation:

> *'eBay? Really? I sell quality products for a high-unit price. What will I learn from the online equivalent of a second-hand market stall?'*

Hmmm. Methinks Nishad needs to take a fresh look. These days eBay sells considerably more new products than used and the range in terms of price and demographics is vast. Fancy a shiny new Rolex for upwards of $20,000? You'll find a few.

But testing sales on such a platform is more far-reaching than merely building knowledge about price. You'll soon find out what questions prospective buyers have; what forms of reassurance they look for; what speed of response they demand and what they want that you may not have considered.

Once you know you've struck a nerve, you can hit the accelerator on launching your idea.

Talk less, listen more

So there you are in your third bedroom, your start-up office, burning the midnight oil, working out exactly how you're going to engage your customers and promote your product or service.

In that scenario, frequently what happens is that you'll focus far too much on what you think you need to say and what you think the world is waiting for, as opposed to what people are actually looking for.

I often meet individuals who are spending a long time developing their propositions – their sales pitch – but are doing it without enough consideration of the actual needs of the people they were going to do business with. Or that they hope they are going to business with.

When you're focused on what *you believe* is the product or service you're offering, you can become distanced from the language and the issues that people are actually thinking and talking about. A very valuable exercise is to talk a lot less and listen a lot more.

An exercise I recommend is to imagine you are sitting quietly in a café when the table next to you is taken by a group of four to six people, all of whom fit your picture of an ideal customer. Precisely the kind of people who will buy your product or service.

They're at the table right next to you, easily within earshot.

The challenge is for you to determine the sort of conversations, the particular kind of comments among the group, that would inspire you to jump to your feet and exclaim, 'I can help you with that!' or 'I've got just what you need!'

What are the words being used by these people that would clearly signal they're looking for your product or service?

Going through this sort of exercise and trying to imagine language for the kind of things people are using in the real world will help clarify the messaging you need to use to engage fully with your prospects.

Let me give you an example.

I was recently working with a life coach, helping her grow her business in what seemed like an overcrowded marketplace, one where having a point of difference was challenging, but vital.

Mary was engrossed in the systems and processes that she used in her work and was increasingly frustrated that when meeting new people at networking events or social events, it was hard to get into any meaningful conversation. She was passionate about the training she'd done, the worksheets she used and the processes she followed, but it seemed the outside world wasn't.

We went through the little 'café-conversations exercise' and soon realised that the kind of issues that people were discussing and that indeed were keeping them awake at nights were around stress caused by feeling overwhelmed by family life and a general lack of clarity around how to get everything done.

She realised her target market were suffering from poor sleep, grumpiness and frustration about things such as how to juggle work and family, how to maintain fulfilment when everyone else seemed to demand priority and so on.

They were concerned about how this made them cranky and abrupt with their children and impatient with their partners and friends. All because, Mary realised, they didn't have the skills and knowledge to manage their lives a little better and establish boundaries to allow some personal protection.

By going through this process, Mary concluded that the way into conversation was to start where people were, not where she thought they needed to be. Once the dialogue was open and the conversation flowing, she could then guide people to the solution.

Simply by shifting from talking about her qualifications and life-coaching program to talking about how she helps parents reclaim their lives and energy, she was able to connect with a fertile market. Pardon the pun.

Way too many soloists promote their skills and experience and systems and processes and modalities and degrees and . . . no-one is listening.

CAFÉ CONVERSATIONS

Your turn to play. Imagine you're seated in your favourite café and at the next table is a group of people whom you consider to belong to your target market. They're having a lively conversation and you're there thinking just how you could help them. What are the kinds of comments you overhear?

List half a dozen or so and remember how real people talk and use their language, not yours.

1.
2.
3.
4.
5.
6.

9.

Identify Your Ideal Customer

Lessons from the world of dating

To get us right into the topic of ideal clients, let's draw a parallel with the world of dating and how to attract your perfect life partner.

Whether or not you've had any first-hand experience of online dating, just imagine you're sitting down now and compiling your own profile, one that would appeal to the person of your dreams.

If I were doing it, I'd certainly say more than 'Hey, I'm looking for a woman!'

And yet, many soloists make somewhat desperate, unspecific pleas in the misguided belief that when it comes to getting noticed a broad, general message is better than a narrow, targeted approach.

The business equivalent is the mindset of targeting 'anyone with a credit card'.

Robyn Haydon helps businesses and individuals put together compelling proposals, and in this comment confirms the whole 'specialist' positioning very clearly:

> *'Customers hire experts; people who can do things that they can't. As a soloist and a gun for hire, you're both more likely to be hired, and to be hired at a premium rate, if you are an expert in your field.'*

People rarely connect emotionally to broad messages. And without a specific hook to latch on to, it's hard for people to pass on your proposition to anyone else. So not only does your marketing fall flat, but you miss out on the gold of word-of-mouth referrals, where others do your selling for you.

Some months back I spent some time reviewing the website of a newbie graphic designer. As I expected, it was a lovely-looking website and slap bang in the middle of the homepage – quite encouragingly – was a short video with our designer front and centre.

So far so good. Sadly though, the video began with the message, 'We do the lot. Whatever graphic design you want, we do it.' And boy, did they do everything! They did the works: brochures, websites, window decals, flyers and business cards, for every kind of business imaginable.

What looked at the outset like a specialised, highly creative designer, quickly turned into an online print and graphics shop. And this was a designer who had asked me for help as he was getting dull briefs from cheapskate customers. And he couldn't work out why!

As soloists, suggesting we are all things to all people is a no-no. Instead we need to position ourselves as specialists and know precisely what we do and for whom. Only then can we picture our ideal clients and have a hope of attracting them.

Back then to the world of dating. Imagine if in your profile you described in detail your ideal partner; imagine you used words and phrases that showed your understanding of that kind of person. Imagine if someone reading got the distinct feeling you were talking to *them*.

'OMG he's talking about me, to me!'

'That's so me! I'm absolutely like that!'

In your solo business, this is precisely what's possible. And it really works.

Stop doing the wrong work for the wrong people

'Help! How did I end up here?'

Sally Burgess started her own business when she left her job as a local government communications manager to have her first child. Let's look at why she spoke those words to me in a coaching session less than a year later.

Sally loved writing and embraced soloism as a way to get the flexibility she needed. However, at the beginning she wasn't particularly clear about who she wanted to work with.

Things started off really well. Her old employer immediately hired her for a day a week to continue working on a weekly newsletter she'd been writing, and they even paid her proportionately more money than she'd been earning as an employee – not a massive increase but not bad, and the work was easy.

A few weeks later, Sally got another gig thanks again to a contact within her old government circles and she secured another day of work each week.

And so it continued. Three days work a week and the remainder spent with Lily, her daughter. All hunky-dory until Sally realised she wasn't advancing at all. Work that was easy quickly became dull. Sally wasn't being stretched, and she felt unfulfilled, uninspired and flat as a tack.

She'd done nothing to position and promote herself in a way that would attract better work, and felt as if she'd traded a job within a vibrant, exciting office for a lonely, unexciting job based in her spare room.

It's fair enough to go for the low-hanging fruit at times when there's a lot going on outside your work life. Perhaps you're keen to travel or, like Sally, are a new parent, but it's important to recognise when you need more stimulation from your work, and then do something about it.

The first step is identifying who your ideal clients are (that is, who you *want* to work with) and what projects you like the best.

All too often, though, soloists are totally indiscriminate about who they work for, putting no thought into who they want to work with and only thinking of their target market in terms of broad sectors.

When quizzed about their ideal clients, they typically respond with phrases like 'large corporations', 'small businesses', 'managers' or worse, 'anyone who'll pay me!'

In business we're more likely to succeed if we know a great deal about who we are pursuing and why.

Once you've worked out the characteristics of your ideal customer, you can then seek out ways of attracting them. Not surprisingly, the best time to develop a profile of an ideal client is right at the start of your business, and the second-best time is right now.

So let's get to work.

YOUR IDEAL CLIENT PROFILE

What follows are a number of headings and your assignment is to add responses under each. One thing to remember with an ideal-client profile is that this can quickly become a key component of your solo-business strategy. When you have clarity regarding whom you serve and why, you'll find decision-making becomes much easier and your ability to focus increases as you are more equipped to concentrate on the aspects of your work that matter. This profile should be something you refer back to regularly and refine as you move forward.

FAVOURITE PROJECTS:

- What is the nature of the work you wish to undertake ideally? Aim high here, concentrate on the work you *truly* want to do, not necessarily the myriad things you *could* do.

WHAT MY IDEAL CLIENTS DO:

- Create a snapshot of your customer's life or work – those activities that are relevant to your products or services. For example, a personal trainer may answer this with a comment like 'they're living busy, inner-city lives and struggling to prioritise their health'. A fashion retailer may say 'they are 35–45 year old women juggling work and family'.

The more detail you can add, the better.

PARTICULAR FAVOURITES:

- What are some of the behaviours and personality traits of those you really enjoy being around? Remember back to the 'Café Conversations' exercise. Think of those people.

CHARACTERISTICS:

- Time to get a little more personal and drill down further. It may help to think of family and friends for a moment – what characteristics attract you? What quality in someone really pleases and inspires you?

WHAT THEY'RE NOT:

- The flip side! What don't you want around you? It may help to read what I wrote as a response in my first ideal-client profile:

'They're not highly stressed, irrational or financially disorganised. I've spent time with such businesses and find it impossible to do my best work with them.'

HOW THEY RESPOND TO ME:

- An often overlooked but key ingredient of a great customer relationship is how people react to you. I enjoy working with interested, willing, engaged customers. How about you?

HOW THEY TREAT ME:

- How quickly would you like your invoices settled? Do you like being pushed around on price? How do you feel when appointments are not respected? Get the idea? Detail your 'first thoughts' on how you'd like it to be.

Handling leads outside your niche

When you start to refine a profile of your ideal client you may find yourself getting a little anxious about closing the door on other opportunities, those outside your core focus. Let's quickly look at that.

By narrowing your focus it's inevitable that your customer proposition – the words you use in your marketing – become increasingly compelling and clear to the right buyer. The result of this is that you will attract a core group of quality prospects, and they in turn will refer you to other people just like them.

But let's imagine you've built your business and created your website, and then you notice through your analytics or emails or other touchpoints that a number of potential customers outside of 'the ideal' are coming to you and asking for services that you don't provide.

What happens then? Good question . . . and a nice problem to have.

If these new opportunities are too good to ignore, then you may decide to set up a referral agreement with another soloist and pass them the lead, or you may decide to take on a contractor and add these products or services as a new offering.

The point is that you have the choice. You don't have to say yes. It may be better to stick to building the business you want, doing the work you enjoy, with the people who most need it.

I knew a tree surgeon who was struggling to stand out in a competitive area. Business really took off when he decided to invest in a stump-grinding machine. He ended up with a rich seam of new business as a supplier to his former competitors. Nice job.

Soloism is all about having the freedom to position yourself as you choose: you are central in the successful creation of an intentional work life. Your business, your way.

10.

Use Language That Engages

How to talk powerfully

A number of years ago, I was on holiday in the south of Spain. I lived in London back then and flying south for some warmth and sunshine was a popular way to take a vacation. This particular break was a package deal where excursions and activities were bundled in, whether you wanted them or not.

On day three or thereabouts, the morning started with a 45-minute self-defence lesson – presumably on the basis that tourists may get into trouble at some point.

The course taught me ways to disarm assailants and some nifty moves to cause distraction and pain. But the one thing I remember was a tip that translates beautifully to soloism.

If a gang of thugs are making their way towards you, there's little point in just calling out for help. Sadly our media is full of stories of people who did just this only to be ignored by passers-by, each hurriedly moving on, with the assumption 'someone else' would offer help.

No, dear soloist. If a gang are heading towards you, you need to very specifically assign the task of providing help.

'Hey, you over the road in the red coat, help me!'

By speaking clearly and powerfully to one person, the message is all but guaranteed to be heard and acted upon. It makes sense, doesn't it? If you were the person in the red coat, what would you do? I'm pretty sure you wouldn't just keep on walking.

The same is true in our business. We can expect attention when we talk to a prospect in a way that gives them the sense that our message is directed purely at them.

Once you've worked out who most needs your offering, you can begin crafting messages that are music to their ears. And we can use this powerful language on our website, in our marketing materials and, of course, face-to-face.

Consider these responses to the common 'What do you do?' question.

There's the factual, 'I'm a landscape designer' or the baffling, 'I'm an environmental specialist concerned with horticulture planning and its impact on global sustainability', both fabulous conversation stoppers.

Alternatively there's something much more powerful like:

'I create beautiful gardens for people without much space.'

Now that offering won't appeal to everyone, but that's okay because those it does appeal to will be all ears.

You want your listener to invite you to get into the meaty side of what you do, rather than tell them all about it regardless of whether or not they want to hear it. To earn their interest, it's important to avoid jargon and to target your language and concepts for their benefit.

In soloism, as in any business scenario, it's far better to be noticed by a few than ignored by many.

TELL IT LIKE IT IS!

Accepting that what you write may be a little messy, in around 100 words have a good go at articulating what you do and who you do it for. And fear not, over the next few sections we'll get to work on some refinement.

Cut through in 30 seconds

One of the most valuable weapons in your armoury as a soloist is a short, verbal profile, also known as an 'elevator pitch'. It's a clear and succinct means of talking about what you do and who you do it for, no more than a few sentences in length.

It's called an elevator pitch as it's a statement you can deliver in the time it takes an elevator to move up or down a couple of floors.

And the reason it's so important is that the person exiting the lift needs to get a full (but brief) snapshot of what you do and who you do it for, and one that they'll remember.

Meet John Giese. He's an accountant. A little while ago when anyone asked what he did, he'd reply:

'I'm an accountant.'

Oooh! How exciting. Sorry, John.

Here's the thing. John loves working with small, creative businesses. He gets a real kick out of saving them the minutest amount of tax and is practically euphoric as his clients learn to get comfortable managing their money. An accountant, eh? The term hardly encapsulates his unique appeal, does it?

Imagine instead this response when you ask John what work he does:

'I work with small, creative businesses, helping them pay less tax and retain more profit. I love supporting them so that they can take control of their finances and focus on what they do best.'

How much more memorable is that? I shared this little story with a group of around 70 soloists a while back. Afterwards, three approached me asking for John's details. Two were interested in using John themselves, while the other had friends running small, creative businesses and wanted to refer him.

Okay, let's get you started on this. Ready? Of course you are!

CREATE YOUR OWN VERBAL PROFILE

The elements you'll need are:

1. A personal introduction and overview of your product or service
2. An indication of your ideal client/target market
3. A good idea of the problems you solve
4. The outcomes your customers enjoy from your work
5. How you are different from your competitors.

Easy, huh? With the exception of highly technical, specialised businesses, I reckon a verbal profile should be easily understood by a 10-year-old child – and that means there's no place for jargon!

Here's how software developer Pauline Ford tackled the challenge.

> *'My name's Pauline Ford [personal introduction]. I am a software designer [product or service overview] working closely with call-centre managers [ideal target market]. I create software that gives call-centre operators all the info they need right at their fingertips [problems solved]. As a result of my services, call centres run more efficiently and operators are better informed and therefore happier, as are their customers [outcomes]. What makes me different from my competitors is that I monitor usage and behaviour very closely and introduce improvements before being asked! [competitor differentiation]'*

Armed with this statement, Pauline is well positioned to talk powerfully about her business.

Okay, now it's your turn.

Where to use your perfect pitch

Assuming you've got your elevator pitch or verbal profile, that snappy way of talking about what you do, who for and why, let's look at where and how to use it.

Firstly, before whipping it out, make sure saying it feels comfortable. If what you say doesn't 'fit' you well, you'll feel clumsy saying it and others will probably sense that. Of course you can change and adapt it whenever you like.

Once stating it feels natural, you can enjoy talking fluently about what you do and who you do it for, and it will surprise you how speedily the word gets around.

Adaptations of your pitch can and should appear on your main areas of communication.

John, our accountant who works with small, creative businesses, may well have 'accounting for creative businesses' prominently in his website header, on his business cards, on his LinkedIn profile and as his email signature.

An expansion of your elevator pitch should form the core of your website homepage and will likely help lead the search terms you use for your search-engine optimisation.

If you're exhibiting at expos or events, again use the same message. Your elevator pitch can be modified to become a tagline, one you can use to sign off on any articles you publish; documents you produce; intros to proposals you prepare.

'Robert? Oh yeah. He's the guy who helps independent professionals design and grow a business they love.'

Yup, that's me. What about you?

11.

Be the Expert

It's time to step into the spotlight

Success as a soloist demands that you are prepared to stand up, stand out and get noticed. It also demands that you stand for something, have opinions and can talk powerfully and passionately about what you do, who for, why and how.

This requires stepping into the expert space, standing under the spotlight.

Have you ever wondered why some people seem to be always getting the attention?

The ones who seem to constantly be the go-tos for journalists, asked onto radio shows or podcasts, invited into roundtable discussions and pursued to write articles and engaged to give presentations. It's because they've positioned themselves as experts, and experts attract attention. And not just from the media.

When you embrace the expert space, business opportunities and enquiries flow your way.

The introverts among you are probably shuddering as you read this, but I can assure you that claiming this space is not the preserve of those who shout loudest; instead it's about who can communicate in the most artful, informed and engaging way.

Designer and author Kelly Exeter is a self-confessed introvert who these days is doing really well as a speaker and presenter. She told me how she started to build her confidence:

'Experience has taught me that when I focus on trying to make an impression, I just end up looking like I'm trying too hard. However, when I shift my focus to making quality connections, I'm playing to my strengths.'

Kelly does this by openly talking about her vulnerabilities. She shares personal stories regarding mistakes she's made and the lessons she learned. The key point here is to accept the notion that when you connect meaningfully, you'll find yourself comfortable talking about your area of expertise. Yes, even when you're talking under a spotlight!

Once your work becomes the talking point, you'll find you begin to bask in it; you'll enjoy sharing your knowledge, and this in turn helps you stay firmly on the top of your game.

The value of speaking and presenting

We've all felt the wave of emotion when listening to a gifted public speaker.

Just watch a TED video and you'll quickly witness the power of someone who speaks well on a topic they know a great deal about. They exude confidence and have a magnetic appeal. Held in the palm of their hand, you become enthralled and drawn to their cause.

What a wonderful environment for the soloist to shine! Up there on the stage, an audience interested and engaged in your topic.

The thing with speaking as with writing is there are masses of opportunities and lots of places where you can speak and (in case you're already ducking under your desk) a stack of organisations and resources that will help you hone your skills.

Many groups are on the lookout for presenters, and many larger businesses are keen to have experts come and share their knowledge with their employees. A roomful of leads . . . how nice is that?

If upskilling in this area is needed, spend time online reviewing some of the excellent materials that are there to help you perfect and fine-tune your talents.

There are a number of organisations – Toastmasters International springs immediately to mind – who exist with the sole purpose of helping you improve your communication, public speaking and leadership skills.

And I'll tell you something. Once you're truly on your soloist path, doing the work you love for the people you want, talking about it with confidence becomes steadily easier. You may even find yourself enjoying it. I certainly do.

WHAT ARE YOU TALKING ABOUT?

Imagine a roomful of your ideal clients, people you'd love to talk with. What are three topics that would have them sit up and take notice? I recommend summarising your topic by coming up with an arresting headline.

1.

2.

3.

Can I get paid?

At the outset speaking and presenting may not offer a direct stream of revenue, but that's not to say it won't in the future. Speaking may well become a profitable add-on to your business, but for now, let's think of it more as an opportunity for exposure to an audience and as a means of creating opportunities for people to get to know you better and then hopefully talk about you to others.

When I started my consulting and coaching business and sought to help independent professionals get their ventures flying, presenting was at the core of my marketing activity. I'd try to speak at events of 20–50 people at least a couple of times a month. Indeed I still do.

I wasn't concerned at all about a fee in those early days. If I could get my travel expenses covered, that was a bonus. I knew that if I could stand in front of a roomful of potential clients talking about topics that were of interest to them, it was going to benefit me.

Typically, what I would do is have a little handout or work-sheet that related to my topic and would have placed a sticky note on the back of each copy. At the close of my session, usually 30–45 minutes, I'd invite anybody who enjoyed my talk to subscribe to my tips newsletter by leaving their email address on the sticky note, or simply sticking it to their business card as a sign they were willing to hear from me.

Around 80 per cent of attendees willingly gave me their details, and little by little this is how I grew my first email list. What's more, I found on average three or four people would directly approach me to discuss my coaching services and yet another group would snap up my book or coaching products.

Not bad for a free gig!

Just by planning your presentation and moving towards a compelling 'call to action' – get my free report, join my list, buy my products, fix a time to talk to me one-on-one – it's easy to see how speaking and presenting has so many benefits for the soloist.

Nothing to say? Hate speaking? Consider this.

Even if you truly hate public speaking and simply cannot accept it's ever going to be for you, you can still benefit from a roomful of people.

My friend Geoffrey found a great solution for his business.

Geoffrey is a quantity surveyor, a person who quotes the designs created by architects. You know, the one who tells the prospective homeowner that their house-building budget is likely to blow out badly.

Anyway, architects always need quantity surveyors and Geoffrey knows that a handful of solid relationships with busy architectural practices can keep him comfortably busy.

But other quantity surveyors were constantly trying to woo Geoffrey's customers, and so he needed to be both regular and innovative with his marketing.

In this instance it's not so much that Geoffrey disliked public speaking, but more that architects weren't particularly interested to hear what a quantity surveyor had to say. 'Hey, just price the job, stop trying to sell me stuff' tends to be how things roll.

Geoffrey needed to get the attention of architects, but how? The solution came after he started setting up little café interviews with small groups of architects. He quizzed them over coffee and found out what common challenges they had in their business.

It turned out that what concerned architects the most was keeping their staff motivated and engaged, and finding well-heeled clients willing and able to brief exciting projects.

So Geoffrey did some searching around, found some local experts who could speak about both these topics and 'hosted' a series of small roundtable events. He would stand up and welcome guests, introduce the speakers and supply sandwiches and drinks.

In a very short time his reputation grew as 'the guy who helps architects'. Has it been good for his business? Well, what do you reckon?

That was over a decade ago and he still runs the events and also publishes blogs and podcasts. These days Geoffrey's reputation and solo business are stronger than ever.

Just a little footnote to that story. The staffing and marketing experts I referred to were soloists themselves and were so pleased to be invited to speak to a roomful of what were prospects for them too, that they gave their time and expertise for free.

No budgets blown out in that little exercise!

PARTNERING TO PRESENT

Using Geoffrey's example, with whom might you align?

You might approach this as either the host of an event or consider partnering with another soloist to co-present on related topics. Jot some thoughts down.

12.

Spread the Word

Build your loyal following

'Don't count the people you reach. Reach the people who count.'

When I first came across these fine words, I wrongly assumed they were from one of today's social media celebrities. Well, I got that wrong. This quote is from David Ogilvy, who in 1962 *Time* magazine referred to as 'the most sought-after wizard in today's advertising industry.'

Ogilvy is considered 'the father of advertising' and came from the era dramatised so brilliantly in the *Mad Men* TV series.

At the core of every soloist's marketing strategy needs to be this single focus and intent of developing and building a loyal following of the right people. The ones who count.

There's a great deal written on this topic, one of the finest and easiest to digest books being *Tribes* by Seth Godin.

Godin defines a tribe as being: 'any group of people, large or small, who are connected to one another, a leader, and an idea.'

In soloism, I encourage you to be the leader of your own tribe, gathering a following by highlighting your common beliefs.

But, I hear some of you say, why bother?

I define a 'following' or tribe in solo-business terms as a group of individuals who share an interest in the same things as you. Who value the same things as you.

June Daniels is a soloist helping others create their own tribes across social media. Here is how she describes her approach:

'Rather than hunting for people to make up your numbers, you need to find ways to genuinely connect with people to build a community that supports and benefits each of its participants.'

If you're a designer, your tribe might be people who feel the same way about the importance of aesthetics as you do. If you're a health practitioner, they value wellbeing as you do. If you're a mortgage broker, they value home ownership and property investment.

When you are able to find these connections, you will gather followers. It is not enough for these people to be interested in what you stand for, though: very importantly, they need to give you permission to communicate directly with them. Let's look at permission for a second, as it's very important to understand.

Permission can come via the action of signing up for your

newsletter or it may be from subscribing to your blog, videos, podcasts or social media.

The point being that these people want to hear what you've got to say, and actively opt in to hear from you. Unlike advertising where you broadcast your message to people, a truly loyal following needs to be earned, and at its best becomes a conversation between you and your tribe.

When it comes to creating a solo business that enjoys a steady flow of prospects, whether they arrive directly or thanks to the word-of-mouth of others, nothing does it better, or as reliably, as the leads generated from an active, cared-for, respected tribe of followers.

It's an investment that pays dividends year after year.

Why word-of-mouth rocks

For over a decade I've regularly polled large numbers of solo business owners, asking them to determine their best source of new business. Every single time, the winner by far is word-of-mouth referrals.

Indeed in four consecutive Flying Solo studies, each with over a thousand respondents, eight out of ten confirmed that word-of-mouth referrals created more leads that turned into business than any other marketing activity.

Social media has dramatically accelerated word-of-mouth, because it's never been easier for customers to share a referral or recommendation – and it's often broadcast to many connections at once!

Also, if you've ever left a rating or review for a business online, you're supplying what's known as *social proof*. We are increasingly accustomed to using social proof to help us make purchasing decisions. And traditional word-of-mouth is absolutely the purest form of social proof.

In spite of its proven effectiveness, what I find surprising, shocking even, is that only a small number of soloists do anything to *actively* promote the incidence of word-of-mouth.

Instead they simply wait for the phone to ring. This is madness.

I want to inspire you to act differently. To get started, let's get really clear on the *real* value. Because, trust me, word-of-mouth truly is the gift that keeps on giving!

Referrals make you feel good

When someone talks positively about you to someone else, it's a sign you must be doing something right and it's a clear vote of confidence. Don't ignore it; bask in it. Referrals make you feel good and so they should.

Word-of-mouth is free

Referrals cost you nothing. In the vast majority of cases, people refer you not because they're going to get a commission, but because they support what you do and enjoy connecting people. It makes *them* feel good too.

Conversion rates are high

A referral often converts into business because a good chunk of the selling has been done. Assuming you've got your elevator pitch sorted and have articulated your ideal client, you shouldn't be surprised when that's precisely who turns up.

Marketing that saves you time

With word-of-mouth you're letting the quality of your work speak for itself, which means you're hardly involved in the selling or negotiating process and you'll be cutting down on the time spent marketing, answering questions, building new relationships and so on. And time, in a solo business, is our most precious commodity.

Rejoice! The serial referrer

A person who refers you rarely does it just the once. Just think of someone you refer and I'll wager you've done it numerous times.

Tech entrepreneur Theo Papoulous made this comment on a Flying Solo forum post:

> 'Happy customers and great service were my number one priority when we launched the service. I followed up every enquiry and made sure customers left as happy as I could make them, even if it meant steering them away to a competitor.
>
> 'The result was that customers did refer friends and family and business associates and I didn't have to ask for it.'

Referrals rely on knowledge and signals

If I'm going to talk about you to others in a way that may lead to business for you, I'll need to know who you are, what you do and who you do it for. I need your elevator pitch. But, just as importantly, I'll also be picking up on other signals that are a lot harder to define.

Of course I'd like to know that you're trustworthy, reliable, that you charge fairly, that your values align with mine and that you're consistent – but some of these, let's call them 'foundational elements', are picked up intuitively, at least early on.

The point is not everyone will 'know' everything about you, but little by little, the picture becomes complete and the vibe you give off can play a bigger part than you might expect.

The good news is if you are giving off positive signals, underpinned by clarity around your offering, you'll find referrals will flow to you from people who barely know you, let alone have worked with you.

You may be surprised by how often others say something like:

'Look, I've got a good feeling about this person I met briefly and I'm pretty sure she offers what you're looking for. Here are her details, let me know how you get on.'

ARE YOU 'REFERRAL-READY'?

Consider what signals you're giving to your potential referrers. What are three improvements you could make?

For example, do you emphasise enough the skills you *want* to be known for, as opposed to those you *are* known for? Do you appear too busy, when what may be better is to foster the perception of being available and accommodating?

1.
2.
3.

On the other hand, some business owners can give off a vibe of being too busy to take on anything else, or worse, give the impression that customers are a bit of a hassle!

Create a crowd of regular referrers

It's a common misperception that referrals only come from past customers. Undeniably they're an important group, but to presuppose someone has to experience you before they refer you is simply wrong.

Over the past two decades, I've presented a talk called 'How to Start a Referral Virus' to more than 25 groups of solo and small business owners in every state in Australia. In this presentation I ask the question, 'Who refers business to you?' Here are just some of the responses:

'Past customers!'
'My closest friends.'
'Parents I met at the school gates.'
'Members of my industry association.'
'Other businesses in my neighbourhood.'
'My mother!'
'Random people in my local community.'
'Members of staff.'
'Next-door neighbour!'
'General business contacts.'
'The networking group I attend.'
'My Instagram followers.'
'Suppliers.'
'My barista!'

The responses are so broad and it seems that anyone with a heartbeat can talk about you with others. While that's a huge opportunity, it also presents us with a problem.

How can you develop any semblance of a word-of-mouth strategy when the audience for your effort is so gargantuan and diverse? It's because of this very challenge that so many soloists are inactive in this regard.

Time to change all that!

The solution is to group people together, regardless of where they come from, by *characteristics* rather than *sectors*. Think of people in terms of where they're positioned within your sphere of influence and from there the job is to work to draw them closer.

People start out as what we'll call *the great unknown* – and that's an unwieldy audience! Once some kind of connection and dialogue has commenced, we might begin to think of people as *new acquaintances* and from there *friends*, *fans* or the altogether perfect *raving fans* and *advocates*.

Raving fans and *advocates* are ultimately where we want people to get to. Not all will get there, but the ones who do have the power to open the door to a stream of referrals.

These are the people who help grow your business by word-of-mouth. Surround yourself with enough of them and it's possible to nail your marketing for life.

We all know of those tradesmen, therapists or sandwich shops that have a constant queue of customers without spending a cent on marketing.

That's the power of referral marketing, and the good news is that it can be replicated in any business.

Lara Siu knows. She's worked as a music teacher for a good while.

'There is no better marketing than word-of-mouth referrals – people definitely do business with people they trust, and we trust what our family and friends say more than what any ad can tell us.'

The referral-bullseye technique

If there's one device that I found incredibly valuable in the development of my own business and that I have shared countless times, it's the referral bullseye.

Imagine an archery target, a series of concentric circles, where the word 'Advocates' sits in the centre, the bullseye.

In the circles that surround the bullseye, each of these words appear in this order:

- Strangers
- Acquaintances
- Friends
- Fans.

With this imaginary target in your mind, *strangers* (or the *great unknown* if you prefer) is where a new relationship sits and *advocates* is ideally where each new contact will end up. *Advocates* actively spread word-of-mouth about the work we do and who we do it for.

Often when you think of those who refer for you, you'll tend to group people by business sector, or where you first met them. Much more useful, I think, is a model based on the nature of your current relationship.

The challenge is to gradually move those at the edge of the target to the bullseye, where the true advocates for your business are, the ones who really get where you're coming from and want to see you do well. You only need a few to work wonders for your business.

So how do you get folks from the outer to the inner circle? Happily it's easier than you might think and can sometimes happen really quickly.

The moment you engage meaningfully with a stranger they instantly nudge towards the acquaintance ring. But it's important to traverse carefully. Be patient. Be mindful of the relationship journey upon which you're embarking.

Here's how old friend and soloist Wendy Buckingham gets talking:

'Opening the conversation with a comment on the weather, the traffic, the venue is a good ice-breaker and takes away that "need to do business" energy that can be so off-putting.'

You'll likely already have plenty of acquaintances. They may be people you bump into at a networking event, at the school gates, in the line for a coffee. Once in conversation, you're likely to swap names and share pleasantries.

In even a brief conversation you may glean an inkling of what they do for a living and vice versa. But they don't know much more about you. The chances are your intuition will kick in and help create a sense of warmth. Or on occasion, the exact opposite!

The way to move an acquaintance closer is to show interest in their life and work. This is not the time to start banging on about *your* work, it's way too early. Instead be inquisitive, listen well and look for common ground.

First impressions, gut feelings and vibes are the priority at this stage. Consider keeping a note about what you've learned about this new contact so you can follow up with any supportive comments or suggestions that come out of your conversation. Don't start marketing; it's just too soon.

A nurtured acquaintance can quite readily move into the next grouping, the terrain of friends. Not necessarily friends you get over for dinner or anything, but more those with whom you enjoy a friendly relationship, one where work is spoken about freely and easily. You may catch up with them regularly, may even work alongside them on certain projects or just know that you have common interests and values that are nicely aligned.

Friends are likely to have a reasonable idea what work you do, but detail is scant. This represents a great opportunity to get together and talk about each other's work, to share war stories and start revealing the true outcomes of your work.

The next are fans. These are people who really understand you: they know what you do, they know who you do it for and, shock-horror, they not only like what you do, they like *you*. Fans are on the cusp of being raving fans or advocates, just not yet.

Typically a soloist who has a couple of raving fans is likely to have maybe three or four times as many regular fans. So how do you turn a fan into a raving fan? Someone who is supportive into someone who refers leads and opportunities?

That's a good question and the simplicity of the answer will surprise you:

Invite them!

That's it. Invite them. In most instances, the reason a fan doesn't open doors for you is that they don't realise you're looking for more business.

Saying something like this to a fan can have astonishing results:

'Thanks for your support of the work I do. I really appreciate that. I'm currently looking to expand my business a little; if you bump into anyone who may benefit from what I do, please nudge them my way.'

The mistake many soloists make is having clumsy conversations with people in the outer rings far too early in the relationship, instead of consciously and sensitively drawing people closer at the appropriate time.

START DRAWING PEOPLE CLOSER

Using the groups I've detailed, start capturing names alongside each. You might write the names in a note on your phone or create a spreadsheet and begin filling it up. Each week, try to move one–three people one group closer.

- Strangers
- Acquaintances
- Friends
- Fans
- Advocates

13.

Become a Content Creator

Leverage the power of content marketing

An activity to establish your expert status and help position you as a person of authority (an *influencer* is the term that is increasingly used), is to create and share compelling content. The goal is to boost your reach, audience and reputation, and ultimately attract paying customers.

Content can take the form of writing articles, blog posts and reports; publishing podcasts and videos; or presenting at events or webinars. And for a growing number, it's all of this and more!

In the not-too-distant past, content creation was the domain of journalists. Employed by media organisations, they were society's most trusted sources of information. In this scenario, the content produced by businesses and brands was purely marketing and promotion.

The world has changed and as soloists we can mirror traditional newsroom strategies to create news and 'stories' that educate and inform, while acting also as effective marketing.

Publishing by any or all of these means is not a direct-sales channel; it's where you demonstrate expertise in a 'voice' that suits your positioning and aligns with your values.

The challenge then is to provide information that genuinely helps your audience and contributes to fixing their problems.

It's back to the hot-button topics that niggle your clients and prompt them to look for help and support. Don't be overprotective of your knowledge or intellectual property; generously sharing what you know and stating your opinions is a proven method for attracting clients looking for help in your area.

Public-servant-turned-entrepreneur Dennis Fenwick agrees and reminds us of the importance of choosing the best channel when he says:

'Come back to your audience – what's their preferred way of getting information about your business, and what information do they need?'

By committing to a regular schedule of content creation, you'll be adding untold depth to your solo business, not only building trust, but building a rich bank of knowledge.

And don't forget, once the content is out there and published you'll need to engage with readers, respond to comments and share with your networks. Plus, don't be shy to comment on and share relevant content from other experts in your industry. Being a source of new, interesting or helpful content will always enhance your reputation.

While you can't control the outcomes of content marketing, it certainly opens doors.

For me it morphed into my first book, was the seed for the Flying Solo community, and pre-empted the book you're reading right now.

So far I've avoided noting how Google loves websites with lots of content and pages and pages of text optimised with search phrases. It would be a mistake to ignore the benefits of search-engine optimisation, but first and foremost as soloists we need to create content for the benefit of humans, before Google.

By staying focused on creating valuable content in its own right, you're not in danger of being sidelined when forces you can't control decide to change search algorithms.

WHERE ARE YOU CONSUMING?

Consider where you are gleaning information regarding your solo business. Keep note of a couple of experts or publications that have stood out. This will help you start to think like an expert.

Tips for generating content that sells

Once you decide that you're going to start creating content, the next challenge is getting clear on what you're going to publish and how often.

For now, let's concentrate on the written word as opposed to videos, podcasts and presentations.

The place to start is to set yourself a frequency goal. You may choose to begin by writing a 500-word article every month, let's say.

Get that commitment in your diary, and ask a friend or colleague to hold you accountable. Do the same for them and you've got yourself a valuable accountability buddy.

Once you have content creation as a goal, you'll find this turns up your radar, and starts you thinking about the kind of things you're going to write about.

With your ideal client and their concerns firmly front and centre, ideas will start to come to you, so be prepared to record these thoughts as they arise. A journal – or digital equivalent – should become an essential part of your soloist toolkit.

Here menswear blogger and retailer Mario Romano shares his tips on how to note thoughts and ideas during a busy day:

> *'I always have my best ideas when I'm nowhere near my computer – out with friends, having a coffee, exercising, in the car, on the bus. I record these on my phone, or even send myself a quick email, whatever works.'*

When an idea pops up, perhaps as you read an article or listen to a TED talk, capture it! Note what's stirring your passions. If something has inspired you, rattled you, or given you an 'ah-ha moment', jot it down. You can flesh it out later, but if you don't write down that seed of an idea, it'll be quickly forgotten. I'm sure I've left half my best ideas on the bus!

Okay, so let's imagine that you've got your recorder or journal to hand, you've got your target number of articles in your mind . . . what happens next?

Don't be surprised if the next step is panic. A blank page can cause the most seasoned writers to freak out! Where are the ideas!? Where do you start?

It's not always easy. So let's look at some strategies to help.

Check out your competitors

I'm not suggesting you go plagiarising someone else's hard work, no siree. But look at what others are saying and how they're saying it. Keep a close eye on how their audience is engaging via comments and sharing, and by so doing determine which topics are resonating. By watching closely in this way you'll spot what readers are the most interested in and you may find a gap in the topic you can fill with your own writing.

Dive into the industries of your ideal clients

Whether it's trade magazines, blogs, or published research and the like, get right under the hood of your customers to find issues they are facing that you can help solve.

Read books!

You remember books, real-live books? The world is full of them. Libraries lend them out for free. Read, read and read some more. Just keep that journal handy!

Make notes in the margins of your books, tear out pages (NOT library books, okay?), don't be precious!

Check your inboxes

A great place to remind yourself of what your customers want to know is to trawl the emails that prospects or customers send you, the comments that come through your contact forms or the searches that take place across your website. Wherever there are common threads or questions, there's likely article gold.

> ## QUICK! HOLD THOSE THOUGHTS . . .
>
> The past few pages have surely given you some ideas regarding topics, interests or actions to take. Note a few down now, before reading on.

Go somewhere new

When I'm at an airport and about to head off somewhere, I buy a magazine on a topic I have little knowledge of and often little interest in. Last time it was skateboarding; the time before women's fashion, I think. I find this a great way to immerse myself in a new topic, learn new phrases and jargon and be exposed to stories that I may be able to apply to my own work.

It was in an old copy of *National Geographic* that I came across *autotomy* – the action whereby lizards drop their tails or self-amputate when confronted by a predator. This usually distracts the predator long enough to make a hasty escape and happily the tail grows back later.

That story inspired an article for soloists that asked 'If the going got tough in your business, what could you stop doing to survive?' The lizard metaphor was perfect!

Using blogs, podcasts and video

As an expert in your field, you have some great ideas and messages to share with the world. So the next step is to decide

HANG OUT IN UNFAMILIAR PLACES

Adopting a fly-on-the-wall stance in online discussion forums is a terrific strategy to follow what people are talking about in a specific industry. Similarly you can check out Facebook groups, LinkedIn groups and so on. While you may not contribute yourself, you can eavesdrop on conversations where your target audience are revealing their needs and problems.

Once thinking and behaving like a content creator becomes a habit, you'll be pleasantly surprised how topics present themselves, and how quickly your article-ideas folder fills up.

Zern Liew uses design and design-thinking to help businesses solve problems. And he uses the sorting of precious stones as an analogy to handling ideas:

'When the ideas flow, collect them in drums without filtering.

'Every so often, go through the drums and winnow out the ideas that really shine. These can then be polished into gems.'

how best to get these out into the hearts and minds of your ideal clients.

Whether it's publishing a blog, recording a podcast, sharing images on Pinterest and Instagram or shooting videos, there are many exciting options for content distribution and a growing number of reliable and tested platforms.

But don't be overwhelmed, this is all good news for soloists. You just need to pick one or more options that suit your audience, your content and your skills.

Perhaps the easiest way to start creating content is to publish articles either via your own blog or by contributing to other people's blogs and publications.

Blogging clearly can be a very effective way to promote your expertise and create material that will help your rankings on search engines.

Not only do your potential customers love fresh, helpful and relevant content, Google does too.

If a reader benefits from your post, they'll be more likely to share it with their networks, which acts as an endorsement of your skillset to others.

One of the beautiful things about blogging is how it allows your unique style and personality to shine through. You can be strictly business and professional, casual and approachable, or even humorous or a little controversial.

Blogs can be brief, anything from 100–150 words, or much longer pieces or content series spanning many thousands of words. Another great thing is that one quality post can keep helping people and attracting customers, potentially for years. Blogs are also perfect for newsletters and social media, and can be republished or bundled into a collection that becomes an ebook or report.

Alongside blogging, two other means of sharing your content tailor-made for soloists are podcasting and video.

Podcasting has grown hugely in popularity due in no small part to the fact that people can listen to a podcast while they're doing other things.

They may be travelling to work, driving, cooking or exercising and listening to your wisdom at the same time. As the technology gets easier and easier, for listeners and you, the producer, it's guaranteed the popularity of podcasts will continue to grow.

A good idea is to get a transcription of your podcast, a process that's easily done thanks to many freelancers offering the service. In this way, the podcast can be turned into an article or blog post as well. More Google juice!

When it comes to video, once again the opportunities are endless and you only need to spend a few minutes online to see infinite formats and styles.

Videographer Jeremy Walton suggests we don't forget the importance of humour:

> 'How-to videos are popular because they are full of information that is interesting to users; however, just as, if not more engaging than informative videos, are funny ones. People love to laugh, so if you can inject some humour into your video, go for it.'

Research has shown that videos are 12 times more likely to be shared than links or text posts, and there's no sign of this trend abating.

Videos are also great for your website, to embed in articles, to share on social media, and they are very effective in email campaigns to engage readers and boost click-through rates.

And don't be put off by the process. While you can of course invest a lot of time and money in production, rest assured that many credible and effective business videos are shot very simply and easily just using a phone. The trick is to find your unique voice, your way of doing things.

14.

Essential Marketing Habits

Go where your customers are

I love the power of attraction, the process of drawing people to your business through smart marketing, but what else can we do to unearth new customers?

Identifying where prospects already are and getting among them is an essential habit of the savvy soloist. Don't just sit around waiting for your attraction strategies to bear fruit. Get out there!

Okay, so firstly, 'getting out there' doesn't necessarily mean moving from your warm and comfy workspace, even though I'm a great advocate of getting out into the real world. But I'll come back to that.

To access places where your customers are already congregating, search for Facebook groups or LinkedIn groups, make use of apps like Twitter and Instagram, and hang out in online forums or other industry groups that are populated by your ideal customers. Anywhere you can see a number of your ideal clients in attendance.

These are great places to demonstrate your expertise, show how helpful you can be, reveal your personality, share your opinions and learn just where your prospect's pressure points are.

There is also much to be gained from reading how others in your industry, including your competitors, are responding to these pains.

Here's an important point to bear in mind: research has continually shown that for every person who is engaged in an online forum or discussion group there are up to 10 times as many people 'lurking' – that is, not actively participating in the discussion but still reading, observing and forming their own judgements and opinions about what's being said and by whom.

FIND YOUR LOCAL GROUP

Search for local meet-up or networking events near you or even consider starting your own.

This isn't rocket science. Hmmm. I wonder if rocket scientists meet up somewhere. I bet they do!

The place where prospective customers look, observe, read and follow what you are doing and saying can be enormously fertile ground, and little by little they learn to trust you and respect your thoughts and ideas.

Just to clarify, when I advise getting involved in discussions, I don't want you to start spamming or shouting from the rooftops about how great you are. It's about building relationships, and all good relationships involve listening as well as speaking.

Don't go in too strong, too early. Curb your enthusiasm until you've settled in and got the lie of the land.

We launched Flying Solo's discussion forums in 2007 and fairly quickly one of the members likened them to a virtual café or bar.

In such a setting it's easy to see how an over-zealous, over-promotional soloist is equivalent to somebody bursting through the bar and shouting at everyone. Nobody likes this. It's repellent behaviour and it's bad for business.

Far better to sidle in quietly, take your metaphorical place at the counter, observe what's happening and gradually start to get involved in discussions. You can be confident that before long, someone is going to ask more about you and you'll have ample opportunities to share what you know and how you can assist others.

Also look at magazines, local newspapers and any publications that cover your sector and, where possible, comment, contribute and get involved in discussion. This is another environment where your response to one person will be read by many, many more.

When I started my consulting and coaching practice – aiming not surprisingly at independent professionals as my ideal clients – I'd sit in a café with a few newspapers and a texta. I'd highlight anything that jumped out as having relevance to my target market and I'd scribble thoughts in the

> ## GRAB A TEXTA OR MAKE A NOTE
>
> Next time you pick up a magazine or newspaper or read something online, jot down or circle any topic that gets your 'opinion-o-meter' flickering. How might you respond to the piece? For example, you might:
> - Write a letter
> - Pick up the phone
> - Write a blog post
> - Rant in a short video
> - Reach out and invite someone onto your podcast.
>
> Finally I mentioned I'd come back to the topic of getting out of your office. Well, guess what, meet-up groups, networking groups and special-interest groups exist for just about every topic in every sector you can imagine.
>
> Get in among them. Start mingling. Start talking. Be where people already are.

margin. Things I might say to the author of the piece or anyone mentioned in the article.

I was amazed how often I'd have an opinion, and once I started to write notes the opinion grew and expanded.

Sow seeds every day

Let me tell you about New College, Oxford. Oxford University in England is one of the world's leading universities and New College is perhaps their finest building. It was designed by master mason William Wynford at the end of the 14th Century.

Fast forward 500 years and some bright spark figured it was time to check on the condition of the massive oak beams that supported the roof.

Sadly the news wasn't good. The beams were riddled with termites and in need of replacement. So where do you go when you suddenly need a quantity of huge oak beams? Good question, and one the maintenance team pondered.

Happily another bright spark (they're clever, those Oxford types) figured it might be good to approach the forestry department who had responsibility for the grounds of Oxford University.

And delightfully – 500 years after the building was created, remember – the renovation crew were met with a response along the lines of 'we were wondering when you'd ask'.

A member of the forestry department pulled out a drawer revealing the original 14th Century plans of New College, where a copse of oak was clearly annotated with a message to the effect of 'Replacement beams for New College'.

How wonderful is that? Five hundred years earlier someone had the foresight to sow the seeds to replace the oak trees that would one day be needed to maintain New College. This story is just so relevant for soloists.

So often I see people buried in delivering their work without a thought to marketing. Or, conversely, in a mad flurry of panic trying to find customers, usually after a period of being buried in their work. Funny, that. I've long called this 'binge marketing' and it's the opposite of sowing seeds.

So focused are they on the job at hand they lose sight of the importance of simply sowing seeds every day – taking small actions that build in value over time and help ensure a steady flow of work.

This is marketing at its simplest and arguably at its finest. Sowing a seed translates to different things for different people.

It may be calling a contact out of the blue, just to maintain the connection. Having a coffee with a business acquaintance, dropping in to a past customer's business. Adding a comment on a customer's blog. Following up a long-completed project to see how things have evolved. Emailing a former customer with a link to an article you know they will find useful.

Far better to be a soloist who connects regularly through simple seed-sowing steps than to be the kind who sits at home, waiting for the phone to ring.

Successful soloists never sit idly. Sow seeds to ensure the roof over your head is nice and stable.

NAME YOUR SEEDS!

Let's imagine you're going to undertake three regular actions each and every week, actions that will fuel your marketing effort. What are you going to do?

1.

2.

3.

How to get great testimonials

When you see a queue lining up at a restaurant, or a crowd waiting patiently for a store to open, what's the feeling you get?

Deep down you're probably thinking that whatever they're waiting for is pretty damn good (or at the very least, popular).

And the reason is that you're experiencing a psychological phenomenon that we've already touched on: *social proof.*

In this case, the social proof is where we naturally assume the actions of others reflects the 'correct behaviour'.

They look like they know something I don't; there are lots of them: they must be right. Because we're hardwired for connection we take our cues from others all day long. It's why we laugh around others who laugh, even if we missed the joke . . . or if the laughter came out of a can!

Just read Dr Robert Cialdini's groundbreaking book *Influence: The Psychology of Persuasion* if you'd like to learn a whole lot more about this topic. For now, just believe me, okay?

It's for this reason that testimonials help so much in the decision-making process of your customers. The thinking being 'these people clearly like what this business does, I guess I will too!'

This was certainly soloist Nicole Marsh's experience:

'I met with a prospective client on the weekend and she said that the reason she phoned us is because she liked our video testimonials. To use her words, "you can't make that stuff up when it's on video".'

When you think about it, testimonials, reviews and customer feedback have added immeasurably to the success and power of marketplaces like eBay and Amazon as well as any number of cafés, restaurants and retail stores, so let's look at how to unleash the value for your solo business.

The place to start is to consider for a moment the distinction between feedback and a testimonial. We're often asked for feedback and generally find it easy to give, and yet being asked for a testimonial can be a pain.

If you've ever tried to get a client to write a testimonial for you, you'll know how taxing this can be, even if they're your number-one fan.

I think the reason is that many people struggle with writing, and a non-urgent task like this will always go to the bottom of the list.

The trick is to make it so simple for them that all they have to do is say 'yes'.

And the way to do this is to switch the language you use slightly from *asking for a testimonial* to *seeking some feedback*.

Ask outright for a testimonial and you're likely to get some gushy, largely unusable words that say how fantastic, wonderful and amazing you are. Great for the ego; lousy for business.

Instead imagine contacting a customer and asking them for five minutes of their time to give you specific feedback. An opening question may be:

> *'Before you used my services, were you sceptical? Was anything holding you back?'*

This will reveal possible objections and concerns and precisely the ones other potential customers may have. Keep a note of the answers.

You might then move on to a question that asks:

> *'What was it that helped you choose me?'*

Again, take notes.

This will help confirm what marketing actions or relationship-building steps are working and how.

Next, move on to clarifying what benefits your customer enjoyed since working with you and prompt for real, tangible detail. If you're a yoga instructor, the benefits may be deeper sleep, more energy and better moods. All very wonderful testimony, so push for as much detail as possible.

'What have you got from our work together?'

Finally in this feedback conversation, ask this cracker of a question:

'Would you recommend me to someone else? Why?'

As you might imagine, asking these questions not only helps to ensure quality testimonials, they also keep you very closely in touch with your customers' perceptions of your work.

The bite-sized response you get to each question can easily be stitched together to give you 50–100 words of really valuable testimony.

Independent consultant Janine Hope has cleverly out-sourced this question-asking process:

'I hire someone to conduct a short phone interview with each client. The interview is recorded and sent to me. I pull out and transcribe the quotes I'd like to use and email the client to get approval.'

Nice work!

Finally, thank your client profusely for the feedback before asking permission to retain some of the comments in a succinct paragraph or two and, subject to approval, use elements of it in your marketing messages.

And guess what? If you do it right, you'll get a 'yeah sure' and will have a terrific testimonial. In my experience almost everyone will be happy to agree to that, because you're not asking them to write anything!

Recognising buying signals

While I don't wish to alarm you, I should tell you that I started my working career as a used-car salesman.

Trust me, I was honest. Anyway, let's keep moving.

If ever there was a job that taught me about human behaviour and how to pick tyre-kickers (quite literally) from buyers, this was it.

And I learned some skills that continue to serve me well. One was to always be on the lookout for buying signals.

Buying signals are signs that may just indicate your prospect is close to making a purchase. By recognising them we can likely move in to close the sale, thereby helping the customer get what they want and saving us both some time and angst.

Buying signals represent a subtle plea that's saying:

'Come on, help me buy this thing.'

Let's look at some examples.

Imagine you're selling a coaching program or a yoga course. When the prospect's interest and questioning moves to 'start times' and 'program duration', it's the signal that dialogue has shifted from the need to convince to needing help working out the logistics. The thought process is akin to 'Okay, I like it; how will it fit into my calendar and my life?'

This is a buyer looking to get booked in.

In the used-car business I remember phrases that indicated my prospect was seeing life with a fresh set of wheels:

'I wonder if my family will like the colour?'

A prospect who is already imagining life behind the wheel is a buyer ready to do a deal.

Other signals are when prospects go over things more than once, particularly to do with money. This may be repeating something that's just been discussed, or getting you to go over precisely how your fees are charged.

'Can you break down exactly how much it was again?'

They also attempt to nudge your boundaries with a little pre-sale playfulness.

'You asked for a deposit of $500. Would you accept $300?'

My response to this one would be:

'If I did, would you take delivery at the weekend?'

Many times they did, and if they didn't, they'd come back with a counteroffer.

If your prospect tells you your charges are too much, surprisingly this often indicates a near-readiness to buy, subject to some more convincing on the basis of value.

A good response to questions of this kind may be something like:

'If my work saved you twice my fee, would that be good value?'

Recognising buying signals and knowing when to close the sale can take time to master, and it's possible you'll get it wrong now and then.

Accountant Jen Fitzgerald has developed a strategy around the observation of buying signals that clearly works for her:

'We have regular follow-up contacts including event invitations. We pick up on signals and track them consistently. Keeping in touch and keeping aware at every opportunity is the key in our field.'

As Jen suggests, the key is to be on the lookout and listen carefully to what prospects are actually saying, and not miss the hidden messages.

SEEKING YOUR SIGNALS

What are some of the words and phrases your prospects may use to signify they're ready to buy? Write some down and be sure to listen out for these buying signals and for more.

15.

Get the Fees You Deserve

Your money AND your life

Questions about what to charge, how to invoice, cashflow and bad debts are crucial, but let's start by looking at your relationship with money.

Attitudes to money vary greatly.

Firstly there are the folks who dive into soloism without really considering the money side a great deal. While this behaviour may seem a little bizarre, it's likely that passion is the culprit. Who wants to listen to the boring voice of financial reason when passion and excitement are screaming from the rooftops? I'll all for harnessing positive momentum, but 'She'll be right!' isn't a financial strategy I support or recommend!

Secondly we have those who feel tied to unsatisfying but

well-paid jobs and are paralysed by fear they won't earn 'enough' as a soloist to replace their wage.

The fat salary can act as golden handcuffs, and it gets harder to make the leap to soloism the higher you go up the ladder.

Frankly, unless you're independently wealthy, your journey to professional autonomy may well require you to make financial sacrifices and take risks, particularly during the start-up phase.

Clearly coming to terms with this early discomfort is not for the faint-hearted, and an ideal scenario is most certainly a reserve of funds that will see you through until revenue builds.

My own experience and one that's mirrored by many of the soloists I meet is that what may be lost in terms of the salary package of a 'proper job' is gained in improved relationships, health and lifestyle.

And don't forget that if you're not ready to quit your day job completely, you can consider starting a side business as we discussed on page 14.

Richard Branson is a great supporter of this approach. In his book, *Business Stripped Bare*, he talks about using evenings and weekends to find out if you have what it takes, and that's not bad advice!

Dipping your toe in allows you to gauge interest, test demand and pricing, and experiment with marketing and promotion. All before you quit your day job.

Finally, before we explore tangible ways to get the most from what you do and how to be rewarded well for doing meaningful work, let me tell you about the work of Ryan Howell, Associate Professor of Psychology at San Francisco State University.

In 2014 he took a close look at a decade's worth of money

versus happiness research and found that while the wealthy often splurged on material items (think jewellery, houses, cars, boats, planes etc.) in the belief it would make them happier, it didn't. As he summarised, it was what they did with their time, how they 'experienced' life, that made the difference:

> 'People think that experiences are only going to provide tempo-rary happiness, but they actually provide both more happiness and more lasting value.'

So you can have your money AND your life.

The economics of generalist versus specialist

In case you've missed it, the benefit of positioning yourself as a specialist is one of my pet topics. This is not the first time I've mentioned it and it won't be the last.

Whether you're in start-up mode, or are someone who has been a soloist for years, it's valuable, financially and other-wise, to be known for *specific* skills, rather than being seen as someone capable of just about anything.

The freelance copywriter is the generalist. The 'writer for fast-growth tech companies' is the specialist. The personal trainer is the generalist. The 'fitness coach for new mums' is the specialist.

Now take a guess as to who charges a premium? Whose calendar is booked up, whose opinion is more sought after and who is talked about more? It's always the specialist.

Solo web developer Deanna Barker clearly felt the power that comes with the 'expert position' when she said:

'Yesterday I had to re-state my specialist area, to explain to an existing client why I am turning down his "great" new job. I watched my status go up in his eyes as we spoke.'

Alongside my solo-expert role, I have a little side-hustle hobby as a chair collector. Well, actually that's not strictly true. I buy and sell chairs for fun and occasionally one hangs around for a while so that I can truly admire it.

Over time, I have narrowed my focus and now deal in just one chair: the aluminium group series designed by Charles and Ray Eames in the late 1950s.

I consider it to be a truly beautiful chair. Anyway, the point is that by choosing this from all the chairs on the market, I can claim to specialise. The result is that I have amassed a fair degree of knowledge. I can spot fakes, I know about restoration and repair and I know which models are in demand.

I know what to look for when buying them and when it comes to moving them on; I know how to best write about them, photograph them and market them; and importantly I know how and where to find the people who are prepared to pay the top prices.

Increasingly, thanks to word-of-mouth, buyers find me and I've gradually built a little waiting list of punters primed to buy from a trusted source.

Now that I'm firmly in the specialist seat, if you'll forgive the pun, I've seen customers shift from a mindset of 'can I afford to buy from Robert' to 'can I afford not to buy from Robert'.

And as a soloist, that's where you want to be.

> **GENERALISTS AND SPECIALISTS**
>
> As you go through your week, keep an eye out for individuals or businesses that clearly sit in one or the other of these categories. Keep a note and imagine each business flipping to the other category. What would be the effect on how they are perceived and how do you imagine their value would be impacted?

Understanding value-based pricing

The secret to setting good, healthy fees is to truly understand what it is that you provide that has the most customer value.

A common error in small business is to think in terms of your price, not your value. To succeed as a soloist you want to attract customers who are more 'value conscious' than they are 'price conscious'.

Let's pull this topic apart a bit more.

If you're a nutritionist and can convince me I'll be glowing and feel 10 years younger thanks to your advice, I'll attach more value to what you do than if you simply offer me supplements.

If you're a landscape designer who talks about giving my family a place of tranquillity and beauty, I'll be interested and feel like I'm getting much more than plants and pavers.

Getting paid well for what you do has so much to do with how you *position* yourself as a soloist and the perceptions you set in the mind of your prospect. And, of course, both parties need to understand the benefits of your work.

What's the alternative? Well, it's the traditional 'cost-plus model' which focuses heavily on financials – it cost me $60, therefore I'll charge $100.

Competing on price, unless you specifically position yourself as a low-cost provider, is inevitably a race to the bottom. There is always someone, somewhere, willing to perform the work for less.

Charge too low and you risk your advice not being taken seriously. Charge rates on the upper end of the spectrum, on the other hand, and the customer will hang on to your every word.

What value you do you bring?

Prospects don't naturally ask themselves what your product or service costs, they ask what value you bring. What will the true outcomes be of working with you?

Here's how solo landscaping consultant Eshani Zahir sees it:

'While I have worked out what my hourly rate is, I nevertheless steadfastly avoid revealing that rate to my prospective clients. Instead, I negotiate my fees on the basis of the perceived value to the client of the project.

'In this way, the negotiations tend to reveal to the prospective client that they are making an investment in the project's outcomes, rather than simply sinking money into an activity.

'Through the work I do, I'll turn your rather barren, dark garden into an airy space of tranquillity, relaxation and beauty.'

Keep this front of mind as you develop your fee structure, and think twice before talking to prospects with the language of hourly rates. Instead, move in the world of project fees.

It's time to delve a little deeper.

How to charge: alternatives to the hourly rate

Personal-development legend Jim Rohn is credited with these fine words:

> *'You don't get paid for the hour. You get paid for the value you bring to the hour.'*

Soloists who sell their expertise (as opposed to those who sell products) often fall too readily into the language of 'hourly rates' and in many cases, largely through habit, stick with this model. While it may be fine for some, for others it's a costly mistake.

Let's take a closer look at why this is, and then I'll talk you through an alternative strategy. You'll soon figure out which works best for you.

Hourly rates

Let's imagine you've taken a look around at what your competitors are charging, you've done some calculations to determine what you need to earn, and now you have a reasonable idea where you need to fit on the spectrum of hourly rates.

It's likely you'll choose a rate somewhere in the middle – not the most expensive, not the cheapest.

This approach offers no differentiation from your competitors; you've positioned yourself within the game, fighting for business alongside everyone else.

Quoting an hourly rate risks putting a limit on your earning potential and it can be tricky to increase rates once they've been set.

Maybe you can do better.

Project fees

Imagine you're on the cusp of a business relationship with a new customer. You're at the point where you're poised to start work. At this moment *you* are in control of the money conversation.

In front of you is the job or task that needs doing and your prospect wants to get it done.

Let's use a case study

Jennifer is a personal trainer. Her prospective new client has just said she wants to get fitter and shed some kilos. She wants to come down two dress sizes in the next three months.

Jennifer could jump straight into the hourly rate train of thought:

'I'll train you for an hour a day, five days a week for the next twelve weeks.'

Five hours times 12 times Jennifer's $50 hourly rate. So a total cost of $3000.

Alternatively she could say:

'I'll work with you over the next twelve weeks to achieve your goal. I'll design an exercise plan, I'll give you dietary and other lifestyle advice and we'll train every weekday. For a commitment of $4500 payable in weekly instalments, I'll support you in hitting your target. How does that sound? Shall we get started?'

Language that looks at the 'project' in its entirety – where the client is now and where Jennifer is going to take her – helps distance Jennifer from the hourly rate crowd and instead speaks to the 'value of the assignment'.

As a soloist, looking at jobs as a 'project' also prompts you to itemise the scope of your work and this too helps reinforce value.

Would Jennifer have written an exercise plan and given dietary advice if charging by the hour? Most likely she would, she probably just wouldn't have itemised it or charged for it.

Just to repeat one more time: customers are more concerned about value than they are price. And when you bind your fee with an agreed outcome, people feel more assured that you'll deliver. They feel as if you're backing yourself. By comparison, the hourly rate can feel more like you're unsure of the conclusion and less committed to the task.

Retainers

Retainers are most often instigated by or for clients with whom you've established a long-term relationship. It can be mutually beneficial to be 'locked in' over an extended period.

For example, a search-engine optimisation expert may be retained to undertake an audit of their client's website every month, plus be on call to react quickly to situations or incidents that pop up in-between.

Retainers can be appealing as you have 'regular revenue' from a trusted and trusting customer.

But be cautious, as retainers can also be used to negotiate a fee reduction. And they can lead to regular 'scope creep' and mild abuse of your commitment and boundaries, making you feel more and more like a full-time employee.

Yeesh, we don't want that, do we?

Should you work for free?

Doing work without getting paid sounds a bit mad, doesn't it? Well, sometimes it is, but other times it isn't. I'm not helping, am I? Let me explain.

There are lots of benefits to undertaking free work: it can help you build experience and develop relationships; if you're in the creative industries, it can help you add to your portfolio; it can promote word-of-mouth referrals and can help you test your systems and processes.

But rather than dish out the freebies willy-nilly, it's best if they are part of a defined business-development action.

For example, when the core of my business was working as a one-on-one coach, I'd happily 'gift' an hour of my time to let prospects trial my services. This little gesture also allowed me to determine if I was a good fit and, as the rate of conversion was typically high after such a trial, it was a relatively small gamble with a big payoff.

Similarly, I've been happy to present to a roomful of soloists for nothing, knowing that if I did a good job, I'd leave with lots of new newsletter subscribers and probably some hot coaching or consulting leads. In the early days it's how I grew the Flying Solo community.

So what about the downside of doing free or 'pro bono' work?

Well, it costs you time, obviously. Time spent that won't help pay the bills.

Free work can attract the worst kind of prospects, ones who don't appreciate the value of your work – why would they when it's not costing anything? And free work can also attract the type who don't like it once you start to charge.

So tread carefully. The key point is that free or pro bono work should only be done as part of a strategy. And a strategy means that you lead it and you have clear reasons for doing it.

A lawyer to energetic entrepreneurs, Vanessa Emilio says:

'I love helping start-ups and driven people and in the past I've offered a portion of my legal services for free, but never to the detriment of my business. It takes trial and error to work out the right balance of free work with paid work.'

It may be to build your portfolio, your subscriber base or your general profile; or to test your systems; to build up a bank of testimonials or any other myriad reasons.

Be clear. Establish your boundaries – precisely what you're doing and for how long – and be choosy.

There's no shortage of prospects who will try to convince you that doing work for them for nothing is a great idea.

This is very familiar to events expert Suzanne Dearing:

'If I had a dollar for every person who asked for a freebie, promising future work, I'd be a billionaire.'

SHOULD YOU WORK FOR FREE?

Keep a note of instances where doing pro bono or freebie work may have a place; possibly scenarios such as:
- To build a portfolio
- To gain subscribers or followers
- As a means of sampling a product or service.

Once in a position of strength, ticking over nicely with a steady, reliable revenue, then sure, introduce a philanthropic strategy to your business if you like. Until then, only do work for free when it suits you. When it's part of *your* strategy.

How and when to raise prices

When it comes to ways to grow your revenue, I see four distinct choices:

- Get more customers
- Sell more to the customers you have
- Cut your costs

or

- Put your prices up.

And it's this action of raising prices that way too many soloists avoid.

While not based on any detailed analysis or scientific research, a gauge I use and have observed many of my clients using to great success, is that if when you mention your fees you're a little uneasy that you're charging too much, then you've probably set them about right!

Well, I did warn you. While not validated by any financial institution, I can tell you it's no bad thing to squirm a little when you hit 'send' on a new proposal.

Why is it though that so many soloists lack the confidence to nudge prices up? From what I observe it's usually a fear that by so doing they'll lose business.

This is rarely the case.

I like the way blogger and entrepreneur Yaro Starak thinks about pricing:

'Pricing is very much a psychological element. You need the belief that you are worth the fee, and you need to use the necessary proof points to demonstrate to the world that you are worth the fee.'

A key point to note is that customers seldom leave purely due to a price increase. Departure is more complex than that and more often has to do with how well you look after the customer, how much you demonstrate understanding, promote your 'proof points' as Yaro says and, of course, how well and how reliably you deliver your work.

So when and how should you increase your prices?

The first sign that an increase could be in order is when you can't meet demand. When there's a queue for your work. A small queue is a solid indication; a longer queue a definite sign.

Another indicator is when you notice a feeling of resentment creeping into your work and this may be felt keenly with one particular client. A fee increase might help ease this, and indeed the increase may help ease them out of your business.

And at times that can be a very liberating thing!

Making small price increases can significantly impact your revenue, which in turn frees up money for marketing and business development. This adds to that queue yet again.

One method that can result in an increase is to better itemise and document actions that you undertake during a project, and charge for each of the steps along the way.

Start thinking about 'add-on' services in much the same way a car detailer charges little extras like making the wheels shiny or adding a fragrance to the interior, and be sure to constantly talk about the value of any additions.

Bigger organisations routinely do this kind of thing to maximise profits and avoid leaking money on forgotten unpaid extras. Just read through your itemised phone bill if you need a reminder.

Successful soloists are doing this too. By itemising tasks it reinforces the value you offer and ensures all the elements in the process are not taken for granted. It also helps with boundaries: a logo designer, for instance, could state two rounds of revisions are included in the design fee, but extra changes after that will be charged accordingly.

Finally, a useful strategy and one that I always come back to is to pre-announce price increases, rather than 'drop' them on people as a surprise.

Here's how I phrased my last fee increase to my small band of clients. I included this sentence in a short note, two months prior to the price hike:

'Having not adjusted my fees for the past 24 months, I'm just letting you know that from 1 February there will be a small increase to XXX.'

With a couple of clients, where the relationship was new, I added this comment too:

'Just letting you know that from 1 February my fees will be increasing; however, given that our relationship is in its early days, this will not impact you until 1 June'.

Having the courtesy to advise in advance emphasises that this is a *considered* move. Sure, it gives your customer the chance to reconsider your relationship, but in the meantime you can turn up the customer love.

Not that it needs turning up, right?

I'll give the final words to fashion stylist Lindy Marsh, who followed this precise process and sent me this note:

'Thanks, Robert! My rates are increasing as of 1 July. My current clients know this and they are all staying with me!'

Nice work, Lindy.

QUICK FEE REVIEW

Which best describes your fee structure?

- To be determined
- Probably a bit too low
- About right
- Definitely going up on _____.

What to do when asked for a discount

Unfortunately, soloists are more susceptible than most to calls for discounts and freebies from customers. I guess it's just too tempting to put pressure on the little guy. But fear not, I've got a solution.

First though, let me prolong the bad news a little more as it needs to be said.

If your client is seeking a discount, it points to you being perceived as more of a freelancer or ad-hoc supplier than a trusted and valued partner. When you're seen as being available ad hoc, it's a little too easy to be viewed as a commodity. And in the eyes of consumers, commodities can likely be bought more cheaply. All that's needed is a little shopping around.

However, in a strong soloist–client relationship, where value is understood, discounts are rarely discussed. Sure, in tough times pricing may come into question, but even then surprisingly rarely.

Book designer Scarlett Rugers has a nice take on the topic:

'People are never actually buying your product, but they're buying an experience. They want your product or service to make them feel a particular way and when you lock that in, discounting risks undercutting all that. Discounting says that they're not going to get the experience they want. It's an interesting way to look at it.'

Interesting indeed, and reinforced wholeheartedly by Neil Rackham, the first man to scientifically measure selling and buying behaviour. Neil ran what is still the largest study of its kind, involving 30 researchers across 20 countries and a detailed review of 35,000 sales calls. It took him 12 years.

One of the key findings, all nicely summarised in his book, *Spin Selling*, was that in tough times when money is tight, customers are not so much focused on price as they are on reliability. Is this person or this product going to give me value? Is my money well spent? Is my investment safe? They want certainty that they will not waste money. Which usually means sticking with a trusted supplier, rather than risk switching to a new one, even if cheaper.

Okay, let's get back to the discount scenario. For whatever reason, you are being asked for a discount and it doesn't feel good, right? Here's what to do:

Push for an explanation

The first thing you need to do is bat the ball swiftly back into your customer's court by asking them what's going on. Why are you being asked to do something for less? Is it because budgets are being cut? Is it because your rate is high?

Sometimes they'll have no particular reason and just ask if you can 'sharpen your pencil' as part of their standard negotiation process. Whatever the reason, you're entitled to know and it's okay to ask.

Consider your response

If it is a budget cut, your response should look at what services you'll have to cut to achieve the new budget. A good response may be:

> *'I'm sorry your budget has been cut. Let's look at my proposal and see what areas can be simplified or removed.'*

Take note: don't drop your fees!

If your rate is deemed high compared to others or if you sense you're simply being pushed around for no good reason, this points to a client who is not ideal and who has quite probably come your way because you've set *your* sights too low. Ouch!

A good response can be:

'The fact you're asking me to discount suggests I've not convinced you of the full value of my work. I suggest we find those areas that may need further clarification and chat through them.'

Talking in this way opens up extra dialogue and allows you to make suggestions, guarantees or offers that dispel concern while maintaining your rates.

But if you *have* to discount

What if you really want to stay in the frame or you need the work? You've done your best to stick to your guns, but have decided to do the work at a discounted rate. In these circumstances always show the discount on your invoices.

Start with the full rate and clearly itemise the 'special discount as agreed'. This way you will always remind your client (and yourself) that it's an abnormal arrangement.

Agree on a cut-off time and scope for the reduced rate. Projects have a habit of running overtime and expanding sideways. Cover yourself and leave the door open for further negotiation if the goalposts start to move.

And finally, agree on a review period. If the reduced rate is for a client where a long-term relationship may eventuate, make sure you put a time limit on the discount. Along the way, confirm through discussion and eliciting feedback the value for money your client is receiving, and keep this up your sleeve as ammunition for the review.

Stop losing money!

Research undertaken by the academic Dr John Gattorna into why businesses lose customers found that a staggering 68 per cent leave because of 'perceived indifference'. In other words, nearly seven out of ten customers leave because they don't feel valued. That's a scary statistic!

It's perhaps not that surprising in corporations where it's hard to make each customer feel special, but this should never happen in the world of soloism.

By far the best way to avoid losing money is to not lose your existing customers. Love them to bits. Repeat after me: Love. Them. To. Bits.

Okay, so let's look at some other ways soloists leak funds.

The giving trap

Much as I advocate loving your clients to bits, all healthy relationships call for healthy boundaries. And while free or pro bono work has a place within many solo businesses, there's a trap that I'll call 'the giving trap' that is very bad for business.

Unlike pro bono work that's done as part of a strategy, whether that's building experience, checking systems and processes and so on, the giving trap is where you discount your services or weaken the perception of your value by going too far.

Time generosity is by far the most common giving trap for soloists. Clients should know what you're doing, why you're doing it and how far you'll go. Every hour has a value and clients need to be respectful of this and take the lead from you.

As I'm constantly repeating to anyone who'll listen:

'If you don't respect your time, you cannot expect others to do so.'

For example, if you give a free one-hour consultation as part of your business-development strategy, don't let one hour turn into 90 minutes without saying something, even if you're super keen to hook the client.

Instead, keep an eye on the time and if you decide it's beneficial to talk longer, pause at around the 50-minute mark, make clear you are about to complete the hour and offer your client a complementary extension of 30 minutes.

Use the opportunity to explain your motivation and flag your generosity. This will have the dual purpose of highlighting the value of your time *and* add value by giving more.

Watch out for quickies

Closely related to the not-strategic giveaway is the 'quickie' job. This is when a customer rings and says, 'I need something fast, cheap and cheerful, nothing fancy. Could you have a quick look?' My advice? Don't believe it. The result can be less than satisfying for all involved.

These small 'favour' type jobs are regularly the ones that cause the biggest headaches and are often identified by language like:

'Throw something together'
'Mock something up'
'Just give us your top-line thoughts'
'Take a quick look'

'While you're here'
'Don't spend much time on it!'

Usually this is really code for:

'Can you do a proper job, but charge a lot less?'

While such requests may sound fair, reasonable and innocent –
and on very rare occasions they are – typically these jobs have
vague requirements, low budgets and fast timeframes. This
false economy is a sure-fire recipe for failure.

The first problem is that people like what they like. If they
don't like the job you did for them, their opinion won't change
just because you did it in half an hour.

The second problem is these speedy jobs can end up
taking the longest time. Even if the initial execution is quick,
the subsequent liaising, clarifying and repairing eats away
at time. This frequently occurs when briefs are hurried or
poorly defined.

As freelancer Mike Williams says:

'Quickies rarely cost you any less than doing it properly.'

The third problem is that once a low-quality job is delivered,
all the control and context is lost. Your work won't be critiqued
by others with the knowledge that it was low cost. It will be
critiqued based on quality.

In the same way that people quickly forget a high price if
you deliver high quality, they'll also forget the low price if you
deliver low quality.

There's a saying that goes something like this: *Quick, cheap, good – pick two. If it's quick and good, it won't be cheap. If it's cheap and good, it won't be quick. If it's quick and cheap, chances are it won't be good.*

Remember this when you feel pressure to step outside your normal processes; don't let your client's sense of urgency become your problem.

Think carefully before putting out sub-standard work. In the long term it may be better for you and your client to take a step back and insist on following your regular quality-control process, even if you apply mate's rates at the end. Rates that are clearly identified on the invoice, of course!

PLUG YOUR LEAKS

If you have any bad habits that are costing you money, or concerns that a weakness may exist, jot them down here.

16.

Work Productively

Avoid multitasking and banish distractions

For all the talk of 'time management' (and don't worry, I'll be banging on about it myself soon!) at the core of productive work is actually *attention management*.

Let's start with that old chestnut: multitasking.

Whether you think you're good at multitasking or not, being a natural at something doesn't mean you should be doing it. When it comes to multitasking, the jury's in: none of us should be doing it. Period.

When we attempt to handle more than one task at a time, we're effectively pushing our grey matter to split its attention – and the human brain is simply not designed to do that.

It may feel like you're getting masses done, but actually your brain is jumping back and forth between tasks, focusing briefly – barely – on one at a time.

Research carried out by a team at the University of London showed that in addition to slowing you down, multitasking lowers IQ. Their study found that when participants multi-tasked during cognitive tasks – that is, responded to texts, messages and emails while taking an IQ test – their scores plummeted to a level comparable with those who had smoked pot or stayed up all night. In age terms, their IQ dropped to that of an eight-year-old child.

I can't think of too many eight-year-olds who are running a successful solo business.

But wait, it gets worse.

In another study from the University of Sussex, again in the UK, researchers compared the amount of time people spend on multiple devices – smartphones, tablets, TVs – to MRI scans of their brains. They found that high multitaskers had less brain density in the anterior cingulate cortex, an area responsible for empathy and cognitive and emotional control.

Yikes! Now before I freak you out too much, especially those with young 'always plugged in' kids, more research is needed before we can say multitasking is actually damaging the brain, but I think you'll agree it's not looking too good.

So how do we put a stop to multitasking and avoid anything that takes us away from our primary focus?

The answer of course is to establish boundaries. In effect erecting a wall around our concentration.

When you need to focus on a task, consider disconnecting from the internet. Since the early 1990s 'cyber-slacking' has become one of the key drains of our focus, with up to 47 per cent of time spent online being gauged as pure procrastination.

Unsubscribe from notifications, turn your phone off, shut

down your email. Establish your perfect work environment and you'll do your best work. It really is as simple as that.

Prioritising first things first

'The key is not to prioritise what's on your schedule, but to schedule your priorities.'

Stephen Covey

Succeeding at soloism is not about being busy.

Sure, you can roll up your sleeves and get stuck in to busyness, but success comes from knowing where your priorities lie and ensuring that particular area gets your attention.

Soloists who aren't clear on where their business needs them most can very easily spend too much time working *in* their business, when they should be working *on* their business.

Working *in* your business involves the practical elements of your work. If you're an actor, it's the acting; for a gardener, the gardening.

Working *on* your business involves strategy, planning, marketing or any action which enhances the practical side. Working *in* is the job of the practitioner; working *on*, the domain of the boss.

As a soloist you need to fulfil both critical roles. And that means not being so busy *working in* your business, that the critical *working on* stuff gets neglected.

In his bestselling business classics Stephen Covey presents many groundbreaking strategies for success.

One key strategy has to do with priorities, and is one Covey demonstrated in front of a live audience. You can still find his brilliant 'Big Rocks' video on YouTube.

Covey stands alongside two transparent buckets with a volunteer from the audience who by her own admission is 'bogged down in the thick of things' – buried in the minutiae at the cost of her priorities.

Covey represents the little things that keep us busy as small pebbles, and half fills a bucket, inviting his guest to add the rocks – her priorities – into this visual interpretation of her working week. The rocks are tagged with 'family', 'marketing', 'sales targets' and suchlike and surprise, surprise she simply can't fit them into the bucket as the smaller pebbles are taking up too much space.

Your business's priorities are left to one side while time fills up with small, less important tasks. Sounding familiar? It's a classic illustration of what happens when you spend time working *in* your business and not on it.

Covey leads her to a solution. Put the rocks – the priorities – in first and the pebbles will fit in around them.

And this approach lies at the core of productivity.

To use your resource of time to maximum effect, you need clarity regarding what will get you where you want to go.

These are the things that deserve your time, attention and energy. Your priorities.

YOUR PRIORITIES

Realising that priorities do change and that yours may change as you work through *The 1 Minute Commute*, let's record your top three right now:

1.

2.

3.

Slicing up your time

Stephen Covey came up with another cracker in *First Things First*: a brilliant framework for understanding time by splitting it into quadrants. I believe the idea of quadrants was inspired from elsewhere, so I don't mind mashing it up, spinning it differently and translating it into solo speak.

Okay, so imagine a big, fat plus sign. The vertical line has 'important' at the top and 'waste of time' at the bottom and the horizontal line points to 'urgent' on the left and 'no drama' to the right.

Got it? Good.

This is Covey's important/urgent axis and it reveals where we need to be to work productively and indicates what robs us of this high-performance time.

The top left-hand 'quadrant' of the cross is where you spend time when things are both 'Urgent' and 'Important'. I think of this as the 'Fire!' zone. The scenario where everything is required in a rush or panic.

When we work in this quadrant – quadrant one – we're buried in stuff that's needed right now. Perhaps you've worked for someone who's always in a flap – indeed, maybe you are this person!

Quadrant one is an exhausting and stressful place to be as there is inevitably a number of consequences should you fail to complete your task immediately. Bad stuff can happen.

While the initial excitement of a start-up can be dominated by quadrant-one activity, it soon becomes an energy-draining way of working that's often hard for family, friends and co-workers to tolerate.

Let's drop down to the bottom right, quadrant four, where things languish in the 'waste of time'/'no drama' basket.

Here we find activities that are the opposite of urgent and important. Think reality television; endless hours on Facebook; trawling through images on Instagram; getting lost on eBay or Gumtree. You get the idea!

Now nudge left. Sitting directly under quadrant one is what may appear urgent, but in fact is heading down towards 'waste of time' territory. Welcome to quadrant three and the trap that is easy to fall into. In this quadrant you'll find yourself responding to what appears to be urgent, not realising you're being impacted by the seemingly urgent demands of others.

The little red exclamation marks in your inbox. The ringing phone that demands to be answered. The alert of another message or update. All stuff that keeps you busy, spinning your wheels.

Not truly important to your business and personal well-being, but enough to keep you away from work that really needs to be done.

Without diligence, quadrants three and four can steal masses of your time. And guess what happens when you waste hours down there? You've guessed it: you end up surrounded by urgent and important. Urgent deadlines. Missed meetings. Costly mistakes.

Ultimately you end up flapping around and overwhelmed.

Before I take you to what I think of as 'nirvana' (top right, quadrant two), let me reassure you that spending a bit of time in the naughty corners can be okay.

Creative soloist Nadya Constantinidis clearly loves mixing things up a bit when she says:

'Don't say "no" to those things, say "less" to those things.'

Right, join me now as we head to nirvana, quadrant two. The top right of our cross. This is where you need to be spending the bulk of your time.

Working in the nirvana state is when you know what's important, but you're not hurried or stressed as the urgency aspect is in check and you're thinking ahead. And thinking clearly.

In this quadrant nothing bad is going to immediately happen if you don't complete your work within the next 60 minutes. There's no fire rampaging up the corridor. In nirvana you get to focus on what's of most value to your business, the tasks that will help propel you forward.

Far better to bask in the energy that comes from meaningful accomplishment, than be in a position of stress and panic.

As you move through your day, check which quadrant you're in and understand why. You might keep a diary of how you spend your time over a couple of weeks; I'll bet if you do, you find quadrants three and four robbing you of more time than you realised.

Think just how enjoyable life would be and how much more you'd accomplish if you could focus on work that's important, but without the pressure of urgency.

BACK ON YOUR CASE AGAIN!

If I didn't succeed in exposing a little list of bad habits a few pages back, perhaps they've popped up now? What steals your most productive time?

Proven ways to get more done

A few years ago, on a Friday afternoon, I made the mistake of setting off to a meeting with a prospective client.

He seemed like such a great fit. A creative independent professional buried in the stuff of architecture and unable to figure out how to step back and grow his practice. He needed a coach. I was his man.

Clearly then, sufficient reason for me to set off in my car to pay him a visit and sign him up as a paying client.

Only problem was, it was a Friday afternoon. I was in the east of the city, he was in the north and I'd forgotten it was a long weekend.

The traffic was awful. After 30 minutes I swear I could still see my office in the rear-view mirror. Man, did I get cranky. With myself.

So much so, I called my own office phone to leave a message reminding myself, in no uncertain terms, why I should never agree to another speculative meeting!

Such was my annoyance that I even called myself back – twice – to yell and scream a bit more.

This slightly bizarre action proved to be a much-needed turning point in how I approached meetings.

Why on earth was I spending time travelling to meet a prospect, when I could achieve the exact same thing by having a call or online meeting within 20 minutes?

Even on a good day, just one meeting can waste quite a few hours by the time you factor in getting ready, parking and travel. It's an outrageous waste of time.

Listening back to the recordings of my stressed-out voice helped reinforce my new intention.

From that day on, I vowed to *always* determine if a meeting was truly necessary before committing to going. The way I did that was with my exploratory 20-minute phone conversation.

These days I attend fewer meetings and get considerably more work done.

What's on your stop-doing list?

We're all familiar with to-do lists, right? But what about a 'stop-doing' list? What are the things you should stop doing? Where are you spreading yourself too thin? The aim is to identify the essential, and eliminate the rest.

STOP-DOING LIST

If my story rang a few bells and made you realise you need to make some changes, jot them down.

Work in blocks of time

I'm a strong advocate for assigning set blocks of time to specific tasks and was really pleased to come across the Pomodoro technique.

The brainchild of Francesco Cirillo, the concept uses a timer (in his case a kitchen timer in the shape of a tomato, or *pomodoro* in Italian) to break down work into intervals, traditionally 25 minutes in length, with each separated by a short break of five minutes or so.

The deal is that during those 25 minutes the task at hand gets your undivided attention.

The concept is really simple to use, and there's a plethora of apps available to get you started quickly.

Every time I mention this concept to fellow soloists, someone has an 'ah-ha!' moment.

One such soloist was, Sally Ferguson, a pet-toys distributor:

'Totally spot on! This could not have come at a better time for me. I'm redeveloping a website, managing our PR and trying to be a strategic thinker. It's time to chunk my day, practise what I preach and start saying no a bit more!'

Disconnect!

In order to get anything worthwhile done in good time, you do, in my view, need a number of periods where you turn off your phone and its alerts, pause email and, shock-horror, even disable the internet. Only then can you truly concentrate on work that needs your full, uninterrupted attention.

Be brave. It's okay to step away from the internet and ignore calls. A period of time where no-one can get to you can be extraordinarily powerful for your productivity.

It takes a matter of seconds to change your voicemail to say, 'Hey, I'm busy this morning from nine to twelve. Please leave a message. I'll get back to you after this time.' Done!

It's okay to do that, but as individuals we don't. Instead, if the phone rings or an email pings, we treat that as some kind of priority, allowing ourselves to be disturbed immediately.

If you've shown those around that you're perpetually on-hand, why would they ever stop to consider whether they could find the solution themselves?

Stepping away is not just good for your focus, it can really help maintain your value and demonstrate to others that you care about how you spend your time.

Change your workspace

Working in different locations, even different areas of your office or different rooms in your house, can be surprisingly stimulating. This kind of movement changes your energy and can help set the scene for fresh ideas and creative solutions.

Try working in a library instead of your normal office, or grab a desk at a co-working space. A café or a hotel foyer, even the garden can be worth checking out. I spent years working happily from a converted garden shed.

Think about what's within your reach. Where would you like to work?

ALTERNATIVE WORKSPACES

Scribble down two or three places where you might work for a change.

17.

Avoid Feeling Overwhelmed

Why do we get so busy?

Since the turn of the century, I've been involved in the regular polling of soloists to help understand how their lives and businesses look and operate. One of the key questions I pose is around the challenges in their work that cause the most angst.

Over the years, the responses remain the same. Second only to finding clients, feeling overwhelmed is the biggest challenge. This typically manifests as a feeling of not doing sufficient justice to important aspects of work.

It's not surprising that a sense of having to 'wear too many hats' is an issue for those working alone, but it doesn't have to be like that, particularly when a few self-inflicted pressures are generally at the root of the problem. Let's better understand why we feel overwhelmed.

We expect too much

Bundled with the joy of autonomy can be unrealistic expectations of what you can achieve. A less-than-healthy leaning towards perfectionism.

If things aren't going quite according to plan – maybe you didn't win that last project or sales aren't growing as fast as projected – the tendency can be to pile on more pressure.

That is, pressure you put on yourself to get the results you've convinced yourself you need.

This kind of behaviour can quickly impact your other roles in life: partner, mother, father, friend, and, of course, this simply compounds the pressure. 'My business isn't growing fast enough AND I'm a lousy dad.'

Pressure, pressure, pressure.

We keep piling it on

Sadly many soloists don't realise that they don't have to say yes to everything.

'How did I end up here?' is the common grumble of the disheartened soloist. Often they end up there through doing the wrong work for the wrong type of customer.

Nothing feeds busy-ness and feeling overwhelmed more than the sense that what you thought was freedom is looking more like a prison sentence.

Electrical importer Cathy Simmons knows the feeling:

'Can you imagine if a boss treated you, talked to you, or put the pressure on you in the way that we do to ourselves? It would be considered completely unacceptable!'

While you may not want to let people down, the most important person in this venture is YOU.

How can you possibly do your best work when you're pressured and demotivated? You can't.

The harsh inner critic

No matter what the positive psychology people tell you about filling your mind with sunshine, there's a disruptive voice in the wings that's ready to rain on your parade.

This is nudging towards the world of the perfectionist – one where everything has to be 'just so'. Open the door to feeling overwhelmed, why don't you?

Mortgage broker Faye Denmark escaped the perfectionist trap when a friend remarked:

'If you're a perfectionist you have no standards at all, because perfect doesn't exist.'

Ouch.

Not letting go of stuff

Close to our quest for independence can be an unhealthy pursuit of total control. Of course you want your soloist journey to be *your* soloist journey. Yes, you want to do things your way, it's why you chose this path!

But beware. This attitude can get in the way of delegating and deter you from leaning on others and sharing the pressure. If you're wedded to the trap that 'no-one does it as well as me', well, then you're always going to be doing everything. You're always going to be really, really busy.

> ## CUT SOME SLACK
>
> On a scale of 1–10 (where 1 is gentle and 10 is mean), how tough are you on yourself?
>
> Where would you like to be?
>
> Name one thing you could let go of that would make a difference:

Take the pressure off

Keep it real

I'm not going to deny the power of positive thought. Holding a picture of how brilliant things are going to be can contribute to how energised we feel about the future.

When it comes to creating an inspiring vision, yes, that kind of strong positivity can be great – but we need to be cautious.

Research by Gabriele Oettingen's psychology lab at New York University has shown that reliance on a vision that is not closely attached to reality can work against you.

Oettingen found that while holding a positive picture of how things will be is inspiring at the outset, it can also trick your mind into relaxing . . . in effect, thinking and behaving as if the hard work has been done. The result can be that your energy seeps away just when you need it most.

Instead, she tells us, what's needed is a strategy she's labelled 'mental contrasting' – thinking about how wonderful it would be to achieve your goals, while at the same time paying attention to where you're at now and the obstacles, work and challenges between you and your vision.

When we spend some time breaking down the various stages of our work and detail the steps involved, we're less likely to be surprised and pressured by hurdles as they come up.

Mahatma Gandhi is credited with the words:

'I have so much to do today; I will need to meditate twice as long.'

Sorry, but I l-o-v-e that saying. The notion of being so busy, having so much on your plate, yet prioritising time away in preparation. Doing those things that allow you to work at your optimum.

Abraham Lincoln said some cool stuff too:

'Give me six hours to chop down a tree and I will spend the first four sharpening the axe.'

Perhaps those words that point again to the importance for preparation resonate better with you than Gandhi's?

Remember your priorities

When you're under the pump, some things may need to get moved around. What is most important? What can wait?

If a deadline simply has to be moved, or a priority shifted, then move it. Don't stick your head in the sand and hope no-one will notice. Take the necessary steps speedily, clearly and openly.

Communication is at the heart of healthy relationships. As soon as you know a customer deadline is in jeopardy, speak up about it. And ideally use voice contact. Disappointing news delivered by voice is infinitely better than notification by email or text message or whatever.

Plan what you're going to say, give justification, establish a new expectation and get back to work. The negative reaction you might expect very rarely happens.

Most customers are quite forgiving and simply want to be kept in the loop.

Reset boundaries and review your work style

I'm writing this from my base in Sydney, Australia. When I first arrived here from London, I was fortunate to be within walking distance of Sydney Harbour, that beautiful expanse of water surrounding much of the city.

Wishing to fully live the life of a balanced, health-conscious soloist, I bought a kayak and spent Friday afternoons paddling around while all the worker bees bashed away in their cubicles. What a life!

When our son was born, household expenses and pressures starting rising. My cruisy Fridays had to be adjusted.

Not wanting to totally let the recreation slot disappear, I reworked my 'ideal week'; re-established a few boundaries with those around me; re-calibrated a working relationship I had established with a virtual assistant, and got a new regime going.

I reassess and rework my week on a regular basis . . . and I often repeat those fine words from Mahatma Gandhi:

'I have so much to do today; I will need to meditate for twice as long.'

These days the kayak has been replaced by walking shoes and a yoga mat, and in between there's been gym memberships and a short-lived relationship with rollerblades.

As I write this, I'm conjuring up some more tweaks and am excited at the prospect of developing yet another manifestation of my ideal week.

BALANCE BAROMETER

Write down a three key activities that will help you maintain a sense of balance.

1.
2.
3.

18.

Stay Connected

Work for yourself, not by yourself

While a few soloists may love total isolation and the hermit life, most prefer a mix of time alone and time with others.

Fortunately, there are lots of ways to connect with others, and I reckon that a regular reminder that we're part of a bigger universe really keeps isolation and loneliness in check.

Some nice solid chunks of connection offer a top-up of warmth and comfort, which we can bring back to our solo space.

You can start by joining a local networking group. Just check out your local business associations or spend some time on meetup.com to see what kind of networking groups are running near you. You'll likely be pleasantly surprised.

You can't beat networking in real life to help build real

relationships, but I know those among you who identify as introverts may prefer to connect with others online. In that case, look at starting an online chat group; this only need comprise three, four or five people to start being effective.

You can do this as an invite-only Facebook group or make use of any of the team chat and meeting software that's around. There are lots of free options, with or without video interaction.

Ideally an online group will sit in the background, under your control so you can get the benefit of connection, but avoid being interrupted and distracted when you need to keep your head down.

Checking in a couple of times during the day can be quite enough to give you a sense of connection – working for yourself, but not totally by yourself. And it sure beats talking to the cat.

Illustrator Mark Morrow loves his little group:

'They're amazing people who really care about me, understand my goals and challenges intimately, and are always there when I need them.'

Cafés, libraries, co-working spaces

Getting out and about is another way to remind yourself that you're part of a larger community. Drop into your local café, library, neighbourhood community space or co-working space.

You could try camping out at a friend's office for a day or two and take turns to swap it around.

Consider starting these co-working days with a mini-meeting – five minutes stating what you intend to achieve and check in again at the end of the day to report how you went. Accountability like this works wonders for your productivity.

I've met soloists, one in a very remote location, who have tricked their brains into feeling connected by keeping photos of friends or family around their office and workspace.

There are even apps that have background noise. I use one called Coffitivity which gives me the constant noise of a bustling café. Oddly heartwarming on those feeling-a-bit-lonely days!

Online groups

Online communities like forums and social networking groups are another effective way to connect.

You don't even have to do this under your real name (just in case you'd like to speak openly and avoid your thoughts being seen by your clients!). Informal discussions can be an enjoyable way to get things off your chest regarding any aspect of your life or work.

If you've come to soloism after a corporate career, it's common to spend a few months relishing the silence. But if and when the need to connect makes itself known, be sure to reach out.

Working *for yourself* need not mean *by yourself*.

The power of small groups

Small, informal face-to-face get-togethers, where soloists build relationships and support one another, have long been popular among members of the Flying Solo community – and it's no wonder.

These 'meetup groups' work really well with as few as three or four people, up to a maximum of no more than a dozen. Don't let them get too large would be my advice.

A small group meetup is a great way to connect with others who share your passion for running your own show and who will openly share the joys and hardships.

Your group might meet in your front room, in a café, library or any other public space. It works best when you all commit to a regular set time: the first Tuesday of each month, for instance.

You can brainstorm a series of themes to explore at each meeting or allow the conversation to evolve organically. My observation is those with some structure that leaves room for spontaneous conversation are by far the most fruitful.

If you can't find one in your area, why not start one up? Look online by all means, but this is one example of how a sign in a coffee shop, an ad in the local paper or asking around among friends could be an effective way to find members.

These meetup groups make most sense when members are from the same area. Keeping it local means you can share experiences and tips in an environment where everyone feels safe and comfortable. Also on a practical note, it is easier to organise when no-one has to travel too far.

Child entertainer Agnes Moskovitch continues to gain so much from what she calls her 'mastermind group':

'I've developed inch-wide, mile-deep relationships that have opened up opportunities I simply would not get through more superficial relationships. By carefully choosing the right mix of members, I'm surrounded by others looking to help me succeed just as much as I want the same for them.'

Creating a space where you can explore individual challenges, maintain a strong sense of group and individual accountability and contribute ideas to a greater knowledge pool can really give your business a boost.

While some meetup groups run their natural course, others get richer and richer over time.

I've known some groups to continue long after any business goals have been achieved and often, as relationships deepen, they morph into discussions that meander across family, health, holiday planning and even retirement.

WHO'S SEATED AT THE TABLE?

While you may not have a shortlist at the ready, perhaps a couple of people spring to mind as being members of your mastermind group? Jot down their names now and add more later.

19.

Why You Need Accountability

Who will you answer to?

For a lot of soloists, me included, work gets done more reliably and efficiently when there's a deadline.

If a customer says, 'Let me have the work anytime this month', there's a good chance the job won't get finished until the end of the month. Whereas if it's needed this week, sure enough, it gets done and dusted by Friday.

Deadlines imply that someone is keeping an eye on your work. They are relying on you, and it's this that lies at the heart of accountability.

A great example of this in action was when my friend and colleague, Peter Crocker, published an article on Flying Solo that challenged readers to commit to undertaking a task within a seven-day period. Anyone taking part had to publicly commit to their assignment and give feedback on their success. The results of this simple challenge were astonishing, with a score of soloists getting so much done.

Here's just one example from architect, Nigel Roberts:

'I succeeded in preparing the content for my website. If not for this challenge, I would have sat there either until I felt it was 100 per cent the way I wanted it, or until I got completely sick of working on it. Whichever came first. Now though, I'm happy having got it completed and published online as I know I'll tinker with it anyway.'

If you keep meaning to do some exercise, imagine the impact of arranging to pick up a friend at seven in the morning and go for a run. Unless you're going to leave her standing on the corner, you'll be there.

The fear of letting someone down, someone other than yourself, is a big motivator. Just like missing a deadline. There are lots of ways to add the awesomeness of accountability into your work. Hiring a coach is one option.

Hire a coach

When I started coaching, few people understood what it was about, making it a tricky service to sell.

'Why would I need someone to tell me what to do when I already know what I should be doing?'

. . . was generally how the thinking went.

Telling people what to do is not what coaching is about.

The reason coaching has exploded in the last couple of decades is because it brings accountability to your actions and the results that are achieved because of this can be quite extraordinary.

> *'You've told me it's a priority to rewrite your profile page – when can you block time in the next week and how many words will you write?'*
> *'Four hundred words and you'll do it on Wednesday?'*
> *'Great, email it over to me first thing Thursday. Agreed?'*

With the support of a coach or mentor you can identify your priorities and then ensure the actions support them. You are kept on track doing the things you know you need to do.

Like a sports coach, a professional coach is a partner who helps accelerate your results. This is all about you. You're the athlete, you're the one winning the medals, while your coach cheers you on from the sidelines.

The job of the coach is to bring out the best in you. Hold you to your greater purpose.

Coaches facilitate a system of reporting, self-exploration and goal-setting to improve your focus and awareness. They concentrate on where you are today and what you are willing to do to get to where you want to be tomorrow.

Soloists are ripe for coaching, as constantly keeping yourself directed and motivated can be tricky.

Many soloists sign up coaches for short periods of three to six months to help them get through certain stages or to push to new levels.

Set up a buddy group

Whether you call it a 'buddy group', a 'goals group' or an 'informal advisory board', the concept is the same. The idea is you pick out two to three friends or colleagues who ideally are on a similar trajectory to you; that is, 'working their way' to getting where they want to go.

At the outset you each articulate what you're trying to achieve over the next three months, say, and you agree to meet or talk regularly and check in.

When you do, you repeat your goals; see how each other is doing; look at what's getting in the way; make pledges of steps to take in the coming week and resolve to check in again.

Such groups can be incredibly helpful when it comes to keeping you on track.

Go public

Another option, just like the challenge my friend Peter set, is to find an online forum, social media group or blog where you can report your goals and progress. You can even just make a commitment to a friend or partner and ask them to hold you to it. Tell the world what you're doing, commit to reporting back and even invite others to bug you.

I went public like this with a 'read a book a week for 12 weeks' personal challenge and it worked wonders. I got to read a mountain of books, cleared a pile that was weighing heavily on my mind (and desk) and learned some stuff.

Getting the best from a coach

If you're serious about enlisting the support of a coach, whether ongoing or for a particular aspect of your work, you may need to shift your thinking from the mindset of 'the cost of the coach' to 'the investment in the coaching process'.

In other words, think about what you're aiming to get from coaching and what the value of that is to your work.

WHAT'S YOUR PRIMARY FOCUS?

Let's assume you're to start with a coach next week. Write down in this page's margins the key areas you'd like to work on.

Know what skills you're looking for

Specifically, what do you need help with? Perhaps it's clarifying your role in the business, improving productivity, or some support with implementing business systems.

Maybe you're looking to make big advances in your financial literacy; your marketing, your personal health and wellbeing, or need support to change habits and behaviours. Perhaps it's

---

HOW WILL YOU KNOW IT'S WORKING?

It's one thing to know what you want, but how will you measure success? Consider some tangible outcomes.

- How do you want to feel at the conclusion?
- What needs to be different?

The more time you spend on preparation, the higher the likelihood you'll enlist the right support and enjoy the best results.

all of the above. The point is, be really clear what you want from the process of coaching.

It's all about the fit

The fit with your coach is so important. Most coaches offer a free trial, so make good use of it. Check out their track record, ask for referrals and testimonials. Where did they train? What methodology do they use? How successful have they been in their own business? Are they members of any professional organisations?

But more crucial than all of these, how do the two of you connect? Is this someone you feel that you can open up to? What does your intuition tell you?

Make sure the fit feels right before you move ahead.

Danielle Penfold had all kinds of trouble finding the right person, but when she did her fabric-design business really took off:

'My coach's support and guidance has been fantastic and I really love his enthusiasm and energy, it rubs off on me. Recently I went to him full of problems, not knowing what to do next with my business. By the end of the hour, he had me focused and energised and with a list of things to do.'

Try this little coaching trick

A good coach challenges you to step away from working *in* your business, to working *on* it. One nifty way to do this on your own and promote some introspection and reflection is by undertaking this little exercise. You'll need a pen and paper to write down your responses.

Q. What are you happiest about?

What are you happiest about in your work and life at this moment? Go ahead, take a break from reading and write down the first things that come to mind.

Q. What are you most excited about?

Hmm. Happiness. Excitement. Both good, but quite differing sensations. So what's exciting you right now in your journey along the solo path?

Pause and jot some notes down.

The final question . . .

Q. What are you most proud of?

Come on, no-one's looking over your shoulder. It's just the two of us. Don't be bashful.

What are you most proud of in the work you do and the life you lead?

Stop, think, write.

Now whether or not you took an active part in this exercise, and I really hope you did, you should at the very least have begun to unravel a few thoughts that you may not even realise you had hiding away in that busy head of yours.

This is a very small taster of what coaching can do. It challenges you to pause, consider, observe and take new actions that support your goals.

HAPPY, EXCITED, PROUD

- What are you happiest about?
- What are you most excited about?
- What are you most proud of?

If you can get into the habit of doing this exercise regularly I expect you'll notice the difference in how you feel about your work. Too often we are so busy in our businesses we simply do not take the time to acknowledge what we've achieved and allow ourselves to bask in a bit of glory.

If you keep your responses in a journal (please do!), you'll get to see how your thinking changes and expands over time.

Before I close on this topic, here's another little self-coaching technique that I love. My laptop requires a password before I can get to work and it's set up to 'lock' after a couple of minutes of inactivity.

Straightforward computer settings that you're quite familiar with, right?

My password for the past little while has been 'write 500 words today'. You can probably imagine why!

Anyway, I've typed that phrase maybe a dozen times a day. Do you think that action reminds me of a key goal for my work? You bet it does. As my core focus changes, I'll change this password to match.

Pick a statement that inspires you to move ahead in the single area that is most important to you – in work or life – and make it your password.

Coach yourself.

20.

Handle the Backroom

Know what support you need

Typically soloists have to take on a lot of different roles. This variety is part of the attraction of working for yourself. But the trick is to not take on everything. Spreading yourself too thin is all too common and stops you from doing your best work.

Letting go of the notion that you have to do it all, then being willing to invest in help, will benefit you and your business no end.

In much the same way that most modern households rely on the support of an occasional, or regular, team of helpers – plumbers, cleaners, babysitters, electricians, gardeners, painters, car mechanics and so on – so too does the solo business. No one person has all the required skills or time.

In my business I would find things impossible to handle without the support of my trusty 'virtual assistant'. From her home office, a great distance from mine, Fiona looks after much of my invoicing, appointment setting, travel arrangements, transcriptions and administration. We communicate electronically, speak only occasionally and to date have met only a few times.

Technology like online scheduling, accounting and communications tools can help automate a lot of business tasks, but the support of real people remains popular too. Many soloists work with virtual assistants and, like me, would be lost without them.

Alongside Fiona I'd struggle if I didn't have quick access and support from the likes of Doug, my accountant; Rich the graphic designer; Jenna, my transcriber; Michael the videographer; Em, my yoga teacher and Keith the gardener.

WHO IS ON YOUR TEAM?

Jot down who is already a paid-up member of your support crew or who you'd like to enrol.

Create an operations manual

Whether you call it an operations manual, a procedures manual or a 'how we do stuff around here' manual, every soloist benefits from a written guide detailing key work tasks, and the sooner you start one the better.

But why? Why, when you're running your solo business all on your own, why do you need to write things down?

Well, surprisingly it goes right back to one of the main reasons you started on your path to soloism: freedom. Having a manual brings added freedom. No, really.

Let's imagine you put out an email newsletter once a week. You write it yourself, you edit it yourself, you format it yourself, source your own images, you set it up yourself and you broadcast it yourself. And the chances are you enjoy doing all of this.

Perhaps the writing takes you two hours and the other bits an hour. The writing is likely in your voice, and for that reason you may well want to hang on to that task. Over time, though, you could start getting a little bored with all the other elements, and quite possibly other things need your attention. Things like your marketing or maybe your gym membership.

It's time to get help, time to delegate some work tasks to others. This is precisely where the operations manual swings into action.

'Hey, I've got an hour's work for you. Here's what I want; here's how it's done.' Whoosh. An hour saved, right there.

It can be the same with preparing a proposal, shipping a product, setting up a new customer, processing a sale and so on.

Counsellor Stacey Mills clearly sees the benefit:

'I'm writing it as I go along. Whenever I do a task that hasn't been documented yet, I open the manual and write notes as I do it. There is now so much I can outsource as a result!'

An operations manual makes it easy for others to do your work. They simply refer to the manual and pick up where you left off.

So ultimately, an operations manual makes it possible for you to take on help, or replicate your business, or even sell it on to someone else. But let's not get ahead of ourselves.

In the early days of my business, when I was happily doing everything myself, I'd block out time each week to do my administration and accounting. Not my favourite work, quite frankly.

Sometimes when buried in the midst of this work, the phone would ring and I've have a prospect right there. I'd have to switch immediately from one task to another. From one role to another.

From bookkeeper to salesman in two rings.

My operations manual saved me. I had a single-page checklist entitled 'Handling new prospect calls'. I'd quickly flick to that and know immediately the questions I needed to ask, the information I needed to share and the key points to get across.

So, even if you're not ready to outsource a task yet, a written process that you follow yourself will reduce errors and make things faster and more consistent. You won't need to teach yourself yet again how to load up a blog post, because it will all be there in step-by-step wonderfulness.

The best time to start documenting your procedures is day one of your soloist journey. The second-best time is now.

MAKE A START ON YOUR OPERATIONS MANUAL

A task that's repeated regularly can be systemised. Start by documenting three tasks a week. A series of bullet points or a collection of sticky notes in a flow chart can be a good place to begin.

Collating key actions into simple step-by-step actions means these 'details' don't take up real estate in your mind, and I assure you the first time you refer to the manual will justify the effort you put into creating it.

When and how to delegate

Not having a viable market, or not successfully reaching your market, is the number-one cause of failure in the world of soloism. Hot on its heels, though, and often a more painful and drawn-out demise, is that caused by getting overwhelmed.

What do I mean by overwhelmed? Well, buckling under the pressure of trying to do everything. Trying to fit too many hats onto one head. (See page 177 for more on that!)

Just because you choose to work by yourself, it doesn't mean you have to do *everything* yourself. And in the wonderful world of independent work there are other professionals, predominantly other soloists, who are poised to step in and give you support.

For every hour of 'grunt work' you pass to someone else, you have an hour more to do what's truly important to ensure your prosperity. Successful soloists outsource all kinds of services from bookkeeping to phone-answering services, to catering and house cleaning.

Avoiding responsibility is not delegating!
As you make plans to delegate anything in your business, be cautious. You can't just outsource a task and wash your hands of it. Particularly when it concerns finances.

You need to know exactly what you want done; understand enough to monitor the work; trust who's doing it, and of course think twice before handing over passwords and account details. In other words, do your due diligence!

Here's a simple way to help you figure out what to hang on to and what to let go of. Ask yourself, 'Does the task have high value to my business?' If so, probably best to keep it close. 'Is the task of low value, something that's easy to do?' Get the steps documented; get it outsourced; get on with high-value work.

Soloists who delegate well see the true value in their time, and free themselves up to engage in the work they are best at.

'Doing something unimportant well does not make it important.'

That's a quote from Timothy Ferriss, and if you've not read his book *The 4-Hour Workweek*, it's a great read that bases its entire premise on eliminating as many tasks as possible from your to-do list by aggressively outsourcing.

You may not feel the need to go *that* far, but the book will help open your eyes, your mind and your arms to embrace the support of others.

But do be careful when you get to outsourcing. Choose your support crew with care.

Heed the words of kitchen installer Mathew Watkins:

'While the benefits of creating more time for money-making tasks is obvious, the wrong outsourced person can sometimes require more management time than they are worth.'

21.

Grow the Team

Signs you need some help

Anthea turned a passion for 20th Century decorative art into a solo venture, and it was ticking along rather well when we first met. In a little over a year she'd designed a lifestyle business that allowed her to transition a hobby into a viable online marketplace.

She was enjoying creative freedom *and* getting to spend good solid time with her young family. Very nice indeed.

We met again just six months later and the picture had changed. There was no doubt she was selling more products to a growing customer base, but the resulting activities and day-to-day tasks were starting to overwhelm her and impact her enjoyment.

Here's what said to me – through gritted teeth – at the start of our second meeting:

'This isn't the lifestyle I want!'

The demands caused by her growing website, her social media channels, participation in events and an increasing need for more and more online tech development were wearing her down.

She needed help and support, but with a bumpy cashflow taking on staff just didn't seem realistic.

Compounding the problem for Anthea was figuring out just what role actually needed to be filled. The tasks seemed to be so varied and disconnected.

Making plans for Charlie
The solution was to start a file – in Anthea's case a blank document – and start dumping tasks, no matter how small, into it. Anytime she did something that someone else could easily do, a note went into the file.

She called this mythical helper 'Charlie', thereby avoiding getting stuck on any preconceived notions of age, gender or location.

Over the course of the next three weeks, the file grew considerably with some 40 minor tasks getting added to the list. While it was still varied, a pattern emerged.

Of the tasks that could be outsourced, many were fairly basic administration actions that when lumped together represented around two hours work a day. What's more, they could be done remotely.

Anthea jumped onto a freelancer website. She described the work she wanted doing (which was easy as the tasks were all listed in the file) and within a week had secured Charlie, real name Jennifer, for a fantastic rate.

That was three years ago. Today Jennifer works four hours a day, freeing up Anthea to focus on the creative side of the business, the marketing and, of course, her three young kids.

It's true that in the early days, taking on help requires a good deal of effort. Even when you've secured the right person, which can take some time in itself, you need to brief them, train them, manage your and their expectations, and build the relationship.

But outsourcing almost always proves to be a worthwhile investment over time, and certainly beats the sense of resentment that can grow when your business is taking up unreasonable amounts of energy.

> ### START MAKING PLANS FOR CHARLIE
>
> It's never too early to start thinking about delegating tasks, even if you're in start-up mode. While you may not actually get the work off your desk for a while, there's a lot to be said for building the picture. Simply open a new file and briefly detail the tasks that may one day form the job description of your very own Charlie.

Employee, partner, freelancer, contractor...

I can't think of a soloist who doesn't get support at some stage of their journey, whether it's a once-off project, sporadic help, or ongoing involvement from a trusted source.

Let's look broadly at some points that distinguish those people who could support you.

Full-time or part-time employee

When I think of an employee, I think of commitment, paper-work, paid holiday leave and sick days. I think of being a boss and having staff. And you know what? That simply doesn't excite me. What's more, in my own experience, much of the support I have needed is very project-based – a flurry of work that once completed can run quite easily without an extra pair of hands.

Generally, employees require a good deal of training and guidance to get a project up and running. Keeping them engaged and interested can be a challenge, and they may lack initiative or any real desire for autonomy.

Compare this to outsourcing to specialists, to other soloists. These individuals are already skilled in the work you are seeking to have done, highly motivated and client-focused: choose your resource well and you're more likely to get moving on a project straight away.

Freelancer and contractor

Freelancers and contractors are soloists. Having said that, through various corporate employment loopholes, many are retained full-time and treated just like employees (only without entitlements, generally). In my opinion these are 'resting soloists'. Replacing freedom and adventure with a regular wage and more routine work. You know who you are!

The majority of freelancers, however, recognise themselves as sharp, savvy independent professionals with a specialist skill. Guns for hire. The ideal energy to bring into your business on an as-needed basis.

Take Rich, my trusty graphic designer, for example. He's

done my design work for ages. Over the years he's maybe averaged three or four hours a week. He knows that he has to do good work. If his work went downhill or if he got sloppy or unreliable, there are many others looking to take his place.

I love working with Rich. He challenges me, he comes up with fresh ideas and he's great to have on the team. He's a true soloist, having his fingers in many pies, from signage and online shops to tinkering with custom motorbikes and outdoor furniture.

Soloists work so well with other soloists, and it's inspiring to work with like-minded souls, where each brings their expertise. Motivated, committed, energetic.

Partner/ally

A partner in soloism is the business equivalent of a life partner. There to share in the entire journey. The good and the bad. Not massively common, a partnership arrangement, whether formal or informal, can be a great decision for some.

Some soloists morph into a loose partnership – or strategic alliance – on particular client projects: a designer and writer working together, a nutritionist and a personal trainer, you get the idea.

Of course, partnerships work best when roles are really clearly delineated. You may be a great architect, your partner a wonderful business-development person. You could be a natural marketer, your partner a finance whizz.

Regardless of the arrangement, anyone you bring into your business needs to be a good fit. When you're contemplating bringing in help, think carefully about who the person is and how they'll sit alongside you.

> ## PONDER PARTNERING
>
> Before you move on, spend a moment thinking about who works with the same sort of clients as you. Not necessarily directly competitive, but in a similar space. Keep a note of a couple of names or industry sectors.

Working with remote staff

While there are many real benefits to working with remote staff, there are traps and issues that you need to consider.

Build a relationship

Just like any successful working relationship, open and clear communication is the cornerstone of success, and with remote arrangements, this is where soloists sometimes fall down.

When you have a colleague alongside you, you'll chat during the course of a day and often not about work. Little by little you'll develop a good understanding of what makes each other tick. Over time you'll build trust and rapport and, all being well, develop a productive relationship.

With remote workers, much of this dialogue is either missing altogether or much less frequent.

This can be fixed by having regular voice conversations and embracing one of the many group collaboration apps. Not only are they great for project work, but they provide an easy and natural way to 'chat' during the day and develop a friendly relationship.

I know Chris Jacobsen has experienced this in his tech support business:

'Just like any other working set-up, trust should be mutually developed. The problem is that due to the staff being miles apart, collaboration can be hard to effectively achieve, creating a gap between colleagues. Focusing on the work that gets done, rather than purely the hours logged, is very important.'

Get the brief right

Good work comes as a result of a clear brief. One that outlines the task, details any considerations, links off to any resources or information needed and that lets both parties know precisely what's expected and when.

Hurriedly getting a job off your desk and onto someone else's to-do list is not giving a brief. It's dumping your crap on someone else. It looks like it, feels like it and what you get back won't be pleasant.

Invite discussion and feedback

Over time, as you get to know each other, the briefing process gets easier and less time-consuming, but initially it's good to encourage lots of discussion.

Ask plenty of questions such as:

'Is everything really clear?'
'Is there anything else you need from me?'
'Do you have any concerns about the work?'

And make it clear what sort of reporting you'll expect. For ongoing projects, a daily wrap-up of progress can be really valuable.

This approach will deepen your relationship, creating a growing sense of trust and mutual respect, and will foster an open flow of ideas. And that's what you want.

If you have feedback to give, whether good or bad, do it clearly, quickly and considerately. Something that is heading off-track at first may be simply due to a misunderstanding of the brief.

Be mindful too that if you are hiring someone whose first language is not the same as your own, the scope for error is larger, particularly in the early days. With these relationships in particular, patience is key, and clarity and mutual understanding will increase over time.

Acknowledge and applaud

It's likely your remote worker is a soloist just like you. Working as they choose. Doing fulfilling work for good people. Be the best client you can be by acknowledging their input.

Specific approval and feedback has been proven to be beneficial to staff morale, with one study finding that benign neglect – where work is neither critiqued nor acknowledged – was twice as demotivating as feedback that focused on areas requiring improvement.

So when the work is good, say so and mean it! Shout it from the rooftops. Everyone loves, in fact *needs*, acknowledgement and gratitude, regardless of location!

Managing your crew

Whether freelancers or employees, the individuals you work with will work best when each knows the role you expect them to play.

Yep, it's that old communication chestnut again.

Precise responsibilities should be written down, regularly reviewed and assessed. Start by outlining the key tasks, item by item, before inviting your team member to review and add their comments.

This document may need updating from time to time, which is a healthy thing: living, breathing role descriptions allow for fine-tuning and help promote a proactive and growing involvement.

Be sure to reinforce the ways their involvement has helped your business by announcing new initiatives, projects, wins and plans. People like to know what's going on and if you can show them how they fit into the bigger scheme of things, they're sure to appreciate it, which will help keep them motivated.

Key performance indicators

Far from being language restricted to the big end of town, key performance indicators (KPIs) allow you and your team to have a valid measure of success.

The more measurable the KPIs the better, so everyone knows the score. For example: process four orders per hour; write one article per week; respond to enquiries within 15 minutes. In case you've been on the receiving end of KPIs and view their absence as one of the key attractions of soloism, perhaps think of them more as a checklist of actions. Actions that once completed signal a job well done.

Autonomy matters!

In my experience, KPIs are more likely to be delivered well when we give freedom and latitude to those involved.

GET IN THE SWING WITH KPIs

If you've never used or been on the receiving end of KPIs, now is a good time to grasp their value. Pause and consider someone, anyone, who does or has supplied a service to you. What are the top indicators – those things you expect and need to see – in order for you to gauge their delivery of service to be acceptable?

Hey, try it with a pizza-delivery guy if you like; here, I'll start you off:

1. Find my house
2. Get here with a hot pizza
3. Arrive with the pizza I ordered.

Get the idea? Thought so!

Be clear on your expectations, yes, but remain open to input and feedback. This level of respect produces far superior work and much deeper friendships.

For example, this fast-evolving world of work we live in means I've long since given up keeping tabs on when people do their work. I believe as long as the work gets done by whatever deadline has been agreed, it doesn't matter.

Handling differing personalities

We all act differently. We all work differently. We are all different.

'We don't see things as they are; we see them as we are.'

Anaïs Nin

And thank goodness! Understanding how each member of your support team operates is a learning curve that can take time. Some love detail; others work best on the big picture. Some crave encouragement; others get embarrassed.

For quite a while I've made use of a free online profiling tool called *16 Personalities*.

Each time someone new joins my crew, I invite them to undertake the little test and I let them know my own type. It's proved invaluable in understanding how I operate, and it's shown me how best to interact with those in my team.

You may like to give it a go. And if you turn out to be 'The Protagonist', well, let's just say I feel your pain!

22.

Stay on Track

Protect your mojo

Regardless of how well you've designed your business, there will be days when it can feel like a hard slog. Perhaps routine admin has gone and got all complicated, nice people have seemingly gone bad, and your action list has gone nuts while you weren't looking. These days are inevitable. What's important is how equipped you are to respond.

Unchecked, the days where we feel weighed down and listless (please excuse the pun), can roll into weeks and before you know it your mojo hovers on the ground like a deflating balloon. I've been in this situation myself and met many soloists who have felt likewise.

The most recent was Dave Court, a qualitative researcher. To the outside world, Dave had it all going well. An impressive list of ideal clients, a work style crafted to a T and more shiny gadgets and gizmos than you could poke a stick at. But he was as flat as a tack and, shock-horror, combing recruitment websites looking wistfully at job ads. He needed help. I donned my coaching cape and sat him down.

My opening question to Dave was: 'Where do you get your energy?' To which he replied: 'Energy? I don't have any energy!' and that led to: 'Okay, where did you get your energy when you last had it?'

Boy, did that open the floodgates. Over the next few minutes I jotted down these responses from Dave:

> *'I used to walk three mornings a week. I'd go to yoga regularly. I'd catch up with mates every weekend. I'd cook most nights. I'd read a good novel in bed. I'd catch up with some business buddies every few weeks. My partner and I had a dinner date every fortnight.'*

Isn't that interesting? Over just a few months, he'd stopped doing the very things that provided energy and a sense of well-being. And it's easy to see that their removal would contribute to lethargy and disharmony. Unfortunately, all too often, these kind of activities are the first to fall by the wayside as business takes priority. I've listened to countless soloists lamenting the omission of the very things that help maintain mojo.

It is imperative that you recognise your energy sources as an absolute priority. Spending that time at work is a false economy, but I'm constantly surprised by the ease with which people forego these pursuits to 'focus on business'.

What's needed here is an attitude shift whereby you prioritise the activities that replenish your energy.

Protection of your mojo demands that 'balance' isn't something that just happens at the weekend.

It demands you let go of any sense of struggle over what you 'ought' to be doing, and demands you schedule and fully embrace activities which boost your energy and wellbeing.

ENERGY GENERATORS

Reading through Dave's energy sources has likely triggered the realisation of a few of your own. List half a dozen while they're top of mind:

1.
2.
3.
4.
5.
6.

What are you putting up with?

Try as hard as you might to maintain a clear, creative headspace, there will be times when it feels like your headspace *and* indeed your workspace are filling up with 'clutter'.

And this stuff slows you down. It's like opening your computer and launching every application at once: your overloaded device cannot churn through tasks efficiently.

The clutter I'm talking about can be particularly toxic, as it's the kind which fails to even get out of your head and onto paper. It's the junk that sits in your brain, bugging you at regular intervals and undermining your mood and clarity.

Here's the kind of clutter I'm talking about, which you may not even realise is contributing to a growing problem:

- You've got a box of messy receipts
- Your phone's full of glitches
- Your inbox is overflowing
- Your website is buggy
- Your desk is piled high with papers
- That bulb needs replacing
- Your car service is overdue
- You need a haircut
- Your invoicing is behind
- You've not called your mum for weeks
- Your cupboards are bare
- Your sneakers are becoming a collector's item.

Have I touched any hot spots yet?!

What you need is to free up your creative mind from the shackles of this junk. What you need is to make space.

What follows is a simple exercise that can have a profound effect. I run through this exercise regularly with Jane, my wife. We both look at what's bugging us and get to work on fixing it up. It never ceases to amaze me how things I've stopped noticing are causing her angst. Let's see what it does for you.

Stay strong. Keep the faith.

Many moons ago, as a young entrepreneur brimming with confidence, I poured every dollar I'd saved into the transformation of a disused public lavatory to a contemporary art gallery.

CLEAR YOUR CLUTTER!

Set aside around 15 minutes and get right away from all your gadgets.

Get two sheets of paper. At the top of the first write 'In my work life, I am putting up with' and make a list from one to 10. On the second, write 'In my private life, I am putting up with' and again a list from one to 10. If either list goes beyond 10, that's fine. Let it run.

Well done. You've already started to move the clutter from your head and onto paper, which can often be a great help on its own.

Next, alongside each item on your list write a time and date for liberation. Your deadline to clear clutter.

If the solution involves others, put their names down and let them know what you're up to, being careful to enrol their help and support.

And, you may be surprised to hear that initially it was a raging success.

But sadly, my early wins were short-lived and I soon realised that just because you get a lot of media attention and draw opening-night crowds, it doesn't necessarily translate into a reliable pattern of sales.

Ah, the peaks and troughs of business!

In hindsight, what I should have done was tough it out and yes, held back some cash reserves rather than splurging on unnecessarily expensive audio, lighting and launch parties, but let's not go *there* right now!

Instead of keeping the faith, by which I mean hold my commitment to what I'd researched and tested, I fell into what many call 'the race to the bottom'.

I quickly reduced prices, I introduced inferior stock, I started selling smaller pieces and I replaced a couple of spectacular paintings with a rack of postcards and a shelf of ceramics.

Long term, these measures didn't work. The magazine *Time Out*, back then the main source of art listings, stopped publicising my shows and while daily foot traffic stayed constant, the quality of prospect (and therefore sales) declined.

I closed nine months later and will never forget the remark from a serious art collector I'd befriended during my brief episode as a gallery owner. He told me that he never bought from a new gallery until he felt confident it was dedicated to the nurturing of genuine, talented contemporary artists.

He'd been on the cusp of buying a $3000 painting when I'd replaced it with a fruit bowl. The moral of my story – and one I've had many years to ponder – is to regularly check in with your early research and development work. In my case, I thought I'd covered all the bases, but in truth I hadn't built a sufficient understanding of how certain buyers (the most important buyers, as it turns out) approached and considered a new art gallery. Had I done so, I would have had a greater resolve and kept the faith.

Instead I rushed headlong into a fundamental change to my gallery and it became something quite different. Much less appealing to my ideal customers and much less exciting for me.

Avoiding and firing tricky customers

With the emphasis soloists place on attracting 'ideal customers', it stands to reason that their place in your business contributes not only to how your business performs, but how it feels. However, with the best will in the world, or indeed the most targeted customer profile, there'll be times when you find yourself working with someone who's making your life miserable. And that does not feel good.

A few rotten apples will be immediately obvious, while others will turn sour over time. Let's look at what to do when you find yourself stuck with customers who are undermining your enjoyment and, in effect, dragging you off track.

The problem often starts when you're particularly hungry for business. At such times it can be tempting to take up any opportunity, even when you sense bad signs from the start.

Ask any established soloist and they'll tell you that ignoring that voice in your head (the one that's screaming 'no-o-o-o-o-o') rarely ends well.

But as bookkeeper Sally Jones says, it can be different when you do listen and take action:

> *'It's a tremendous feeling of relief when you don't have to stress out about a job you wouldn't have enjoyed doing!'*

In a situation where you have negative gut feel, at the very least add a 'pause' into the sign-up or on-boarding process. It's far better to say 'this work interests me greatly, I'd just like to give it some thought over the next 48 hours' than it is to accept it on the spot and call up a month later desperately trying to back-pedal.

How to spot the warning signs

The indicators of the 'non-ideal' customer are many and varied and differ from soloist to soloist.

Sometimes it's a simple personality mismatch: I may love someone who makes your skin crawl and vice versa.

Other times, the characteristics may align with one of these groups:

The tyre-kickers

These are the folk who demand a great deal of time before you realise they are only shopping around. In hindsight the impersonal and generic nature of their enquiry is often a warning sign.

Referred, but by no means convinced

Next up are those who are talking to you because someone else insisted they should. These people often come across as unconvinced and disengaged.

The 'you do this, I'll make you rich' mob

There are those who offer you some unusual payment arrangement, ranging from the 'when my business goes viral, you'll get a piece of the action' to the 'help me out on this job and I'll send so much work your way in the future'.

I'm sorry to say, in my experience these 'offers' never come to fruition. Never.

Away with the pixies

Also near the top of the time-waster list are those who from the start fail to get to meetings on time, don't send you the stuff they said they'll send, don't respond to your emails or calls and generally make it clear they're going to be hard work.

They either need to step up (sometimes with your guidance) or step away. Far, far away.

If getting your customer to step up is the goal, you'll likely need to pause what you're doing and clarify how the flow of work needs to run. Often behaviours change when we explain that the end result is in jeopardy.

While these characteristics can help you spot a bad egg early, what about those who appear ideal at the outset, yet head south after you start working with them?

The starting point here is to work out who's changed. Is it your client who has turned bad, or have you changed your focus, perhaps upped *your* game?

Whatever the case, you may decide to ride it out. But if you'd prefer to give them a gentle nudge towards the exit, you'll need to consider the ideal timing, the reason you're going to give and how you'll deliver the message.

Planning is needed, because blowing up is rarely a sensible strategy.

Just ask florist Rosemary Simpson:

'I'd had enough of my customer's disorganisation. I pulled the plug spontaneously and, it must be said, somewhat clumsily. I feel relieved to have lost him from my business, but wish I'd got my invoices paid before I exploded. Next time, I'll plan my exit a little more graciously!'

Let's learn from Rosemary. Try using language like: 'I don't think I'm the best person to work with you on this' or 'I'm making some changes to the focus of my work and from the beginning of next month will need to cease my work with you'.

Such phrases are along the right lines and it may be prudent to also offer to be available for a transition period. 'Of course, I'll be happy to assist with a handover to your new supplier.'

Finishing up with a client can present the perfect opportunity to introduce an alternative provider to take your place – hopefully a fellow soloist who is genuinely better suited – so consider having a referral process in place.

Working out a smooth exit strategy means you won't leave your client in the lurch, plus you can cultivate a good working relationship with those you may have considered competitors.

NOTICING THE SIGNALS

If you've any customers in your business who are edging towards less-than-ideal status, keep a close eye on them. Start by naming them and building up a small dossier of their less-than-ideal behaviours.

Next, consider what actions are best. Can you help them improve or is it best to show them the door?

23.

Refresh and Rejuvenate

When it's time to stir things up

A big appeal of working for yourself is escaping the incompetent or even bullying bosses who make your life a misery. But when you leave employment to run your own show, it's not just those bosses that you leave behind.

You also leave behind the great bosses. The ones who motivate you, guide you, teach you all the tricks of the trade.

In soloism, there's no-one breathing down your neck, but there's also no-one patting you on the back, advising your next move and looking out for your career.

So just imagine you are in a job. You loved it when you started, but two years later, you're doing exactly the same work for exactly the same sort of people and you're getting fed up with it.

The people you loved working with when you started are

beginning to bore you. Elements of the work that you used to revel in now irritate you immensely.

If you were feeling like this, the chances are, you'd go to your great boss and you'd say, 'Hey. I need to switch. I need to change. I need to get promoted. I need to do something new and exciting.'

And if your boss didn't listen to you, you'd soon leave and go and work somewhere else.

In soloism, if a time arises where you hit a wall in this way, it's up to you to refresh and rejuvenate your business yourself. You need to be your own senior manager!

Rather than wait for the boredom to take hold, soloists need to proactively make changes to stay interested.

Not only should you regularly check in with how you feel, but you should also seek out fresh ways to run your business. For this to work you'll need to be brave enough to stir things up. To stretch and push yourself.

Another great option is to seek out an experienced business mentor who is willing to sit with you a few times a year and be your sounding board. It's something I do with my clients and it's fascinating (and always surprising) to see what comes up. Ideas that you didn't realise you had pop up to the surface.

To keep doing the same old stuff in the face of frustration eventually leads to boredom or burnout. And that's bad for you, your business and your customers.

Stretch, grow and flourish

I have a training budget. No, really. In my solo business, my lovely boss (that's me!) generously allocates 1000 bucks a year towards my professional development. What a guy!

What's more, I can spend it on anything that advances my skills. In the past year, I've subscribed to a couple of new magazines – one blatantly business-y, one more creative. I've bought half a dozen books, have taken five online courses and attended conferences on podcasting and online media trends.

Lots of people are attracted to soloism because they can work their own way. That's all well and good, but you need to keep abreast of what's going on *out there* so you can keep delivering your best.

Working alone, there's no human-resources department to send you on educational jaunts. No strategic roadmaps, performance reviews or fast-track programs. So, if you don't make your ongoing professional development a priority, no-one else will.

While I'm not a huge fan of the business he created, McDonald's, Ray Kroc clearly knew a thing or two about how to keep things fresh:

'When you're green, you're growing. When you're ripe, you rot.'

Upskilling has never been so easy and accessible for us soloists. With so many quality training options both offline and online, you'll be astonished at what's available and how affordable it can be.

Almost all industries and sectors have a major conference each year. So bite the bullet and buy a ticket. You'll hear from expert speakers, make some new connections and get a feel for the future of your business and career.

Aside from books, magazines and courses, other means of freshening things up are of course getting out and about.

Taking some time off and immersing yourself in new cultures is a great way to broaden your horizons.

Similarly, picking up new hobbies and pastimes builds on skills and helps foster new ideas and approaches.

Actions like these open up new pathways in your brain and help to create a 'growth mindset' as Carol Dweck explained in her famous TED talk, 'The Power of Believing That You Can Improve'.

In the presentation she concluded that each time you push out of your comfort zone to learn something fresh and potentially difficult or challenging, the neurons in your brain form new, stronger connections. A kind of 'knowledge superhighway'.

So what don't you know enough about *yet*?

STRETCHING AND GROWING

Where would you like to upskill? Keep a note of aspects of work or life that you'd like to bolster.

24.

When Things Go Wrong

Who has the gun?

While it may be somewhat uncomfortable, an essential question to ask is: who or what could dramatically impact the survival of your business?

Who has the gun that could shoot you down? Or less dramatically, who could pull the rug out from under you?

If you've built a business that relies totally on Google sending you traffic, then in your case Google has the gun. A change to its algorithm or business model, and your leads might disappear.

If you do all your work with one customer, that customer has the gun. If they change suppliers, where will it leave you?

Leaving survival in the hands of others equates to forfeiting control, and while large organisations can generally live

WHO HAS THE GUN?

On the basis that forewarned is forearmed, carefully consider your responses to these questions:

- Who controls your website or core-technology platform?
- Could the departure of one person cause BIG problems?
- Are you too reliant on any particular customer or supplier?
- Does your survival rely on another business?
- Do you have a business partner who is showing signs of being unreliable or wobbly?
- Is your data safe?
- Are your insurances sufficient?

As unpleasant as it may be, running through a few disaster scenarios can help you manage any real-life crises.

Most commonly the one with the gun is YOU. Many solo ventures come grinding to a halt the moment you do.

Now there's a topic to take a closer look at.

through all sorts of damage, in this instance there's no denying that us little guys are more vulnerable. But thankfully we have the agility to take quick, decisive action.

I had a 'man with the gun' moment a few years back when our then-outsourced web development team announced they were relocating from Sydney to San Francisco and were unable to support us any longer. We had three weeks notice before they turned off our website (and thereby over 90 per cent of my revenue) and it was terrifying.

Fashion designer Lucy Wright knows this feeling:

'I was totally stoked to have a department store take my range. However, such was the size of their orders that after a few months they were the only outlet I could supply. Before I knew it, they accounted for 90 per cent of my income.

'And then they wobbled. I won't be making that mistake again.'

In tech circles, this 'man with the gun' concept is known as the 'single point of failure', the point at which were one part of a system to fail, the entire system would grind to a halt.

I'm feeling a bit queasy now. I'll get off this topic and rather than say any more will show you a list of things you may like to consider.

What to do when you're not around

One of the appeals of soloism is that it sits comfortably alongside a chosen lifestyle, and this inevitably means you'll want to create a business that's flexible enough to accommodate a range of planned or unplanned changes.

Maybe you need to spend time caring for a loved one, or look after a newborn baby, or perhaps you'd like an extended holiday.

Perhaps you are unwell and unexpectedly out of action. Whatever the reason, you're leaving the flight deck for a while and we want this baby to stay in the air!

Here's what you need to do.

Rely on your systems and processes

You've spent time documenting tasks; now is the time to put them to good use. Start by getting the basics covered.

Who's going to handle the phones and emails? Voicemail and autoresponders are there for a reason, remember.

Speak up
At the first sign that you may be disappearing for a while, let those around you know all about it and be sure to give their reaction and your response some thought before you make any announcements.

> *'I know you're going to be concerned by XYZ – here's how we're going to handle it . . .'*

Go through all the likely scenarios
When you sit down and pull apart all the ramifications of your absence, the likelihood is it won't seem as catastrophic as you imagined. In reality most situations can be handled, and you'll be amazed just how readily those around you are willing and able to jump in and help.

Co-opt, don't compete
In the old days, people would keep their distance from those in the same field. 'Don't share ideas or resources with competitors, they may get ahead of you!' These days this attitude is simply out of touch.

If you've got alliances with those in your industry, they may very well be able to handle some clients on your behalf while you're out of the frame, and vice versa.

Make full use of technology

Automation software, video conferencing, document sharing and the list goes on. We're surrounded by tools to keep the impact of our disappearance to a minimum, so make use of them.

In an ideal world you will have prepared your business in advance to enable you to step away for a period, rather than respond to a crisis.

But sometimes in life, a swift shove can be the fastest way to get things done. Necessity is the mother of invention, after all.

I've lost count of the number of soloists I've known who have come back from an extended break with a more streamlined, efficient and sustainable business.

YOUR 'TAKE A BREAK' PLAN

Keep a note of the people who may be in a position to assist if you were to head off on extended leave for any reason.

If you mess up

Service recovery paradox

The term 'service recovery paradox' was coined in 1992 by professors Michael McCollough and Sundar Bharadwaj from the American Marketing Association.

It describes a situation in which you think more highly of a company after they've made and corrected a problem than how you'd think of them if they hadn't screwed up in the first place.

Yes, you heard that right: customers can think more highly of you if you make a mistake and fix it brilliantly than if you don't make any mistakes at all.

Now before you rush off making mistakes as a growth strategy, I should tell you there's a catch. It's how you acknowledge, fix and communicate that's the bit you have to get right. Really get right.

In your solo business you're going to mess up at some point, and it may not be with customers; it may involve suppliers, or those on your team. Frankly it may be anyone, anywhere, anytime.

The key thing is to speak up fast, talk honestly and openly and to balance the mistake with your best plans to rectify.

If part of this involves speaking to unhappy customers, my advice is to 'respond, not react'.

Do this by firstly listening fully to their grievances, take notes and avoid the temptation to interrupt and say your piece. Once they've had their say, thank them and assure them you'll respond speedily.

When you call back (and you must call back!) you'll be addressing each of their concerns with the heat out of the situation and the two of you can have the rectifying conversation in a more calm and considered atmosphere.

Hiding under the desk, ignoring calls and generally going AWOL is never the way to behave.

While I can't tell you who said it, these fine words work for me:

'When things seem like they're falling apart, they might actually be falling into place.'

Successful soloists take mistakes on the chin. Acknowledge, learn, rectify and get back to work.

As the quote suggests, sometimes, when everything feels like a world of chaos, it may be about to take on a stronger, better shape.

25.

What's Next?

Keep moving and shaking

A good number of solo businesses evolve, change shape and shift direction over time. Sometimes you'll do this in response to market need, sometimes because you want to freshen things up, or on occasion, simply because you see another opportunity and fancy grabbing it. Another joy of being an agile soloist!

The portfolio business

Having a portfolio business means that you generate revenue from a number of sources. These may be directly related to one another – a graphic designer developing a design-training course, for example – or they may be totally unrelated.

You may choose to rent out a couple of rooms in your home, you might start a small plant nursery cultivating succulents from your backyard or you may do some property renovation or investment.

A portfolio business can be a satisfying way to supplement income when your main source has levelled out. It is also a great option for those looking to avoid a situation where they are overly reliant on one income source.

And surprisingly often, what starts out as a side project can end up being the main game.

Is it time to flip?

What many deem to be a business cessation is frequently a business metamorphosis – a change in nature and direction. A 'flip' from one kind of career to another.

I've seen plenty of soloists manage the flip to great success. It may be from consultant to video broadcaster, from yoga teacher to author and presenter, from bricks and mortar store to online marketplace.

The decision to go it alone brings with it an energy, a momentum, that positions you in the flow of ideas and opportunities. It's only when you're out in the world doing your work that you start to really see them.

Opportunities come with the soloist territory, so it shouldn't surprise you when they present themselves directly in front of you.

My advice? Don't be afraid of the flip. If you study the trajectory of practically every successful business, I guarantee you'll see a change of direction somewhere in its timeline.

Rarely does a business go in a straight line from original idea to maturity – just ask Rich:

'I was really quite happy with my signage business, and then one day my best customer (for whom I'd been doing more and more vehicle signs), asks me if I'd like to join him in his commercial fit-out business. That was three years ago. I love the hands-on nature of the work. I now own a percentage of that business and still make signs for others.'

Should you ever want to exit your business

You'll likely have heard the phrase 'start with the end in mind' and how it's super important to build your exit or sale strategy into your original business plan.

While I don't disagree with the sentiment, I'm here to tell you that *no-one does that.*

In a 2016 Flying Solo poll of over 1000 soloists, more than seven out of ten confessed to having no exit plan, with many saying they simply intend to keep doing the work, draw a healthy salary and shut up shop when the time comes.

And that's all totally fine if that's how you want to play it. The main thing is to give the topic thought, even if it's in the form of some 'what if' thinking, as opposed to a definite plan.

When you're working solo the unexpected can happen: illness, a change in personal circumstances or a market shift. Far better to do some 'what if' thinking now than do nothing at all. So let's do just that.

First a bit of context.

In *Built to Sell*, John Warrilow compartmentalises us into three types:

- *Mastercraftspeople:* those of us with a particular talent, loving the very craft of our work.
- *Freedom Fighters:* the pioneers among us who are striving to go our own unique way.
- *Mountain Climbers:* those heading for the top of the mountain no matter what.

Knowing which of these personas you most embrace can, Warrilow suggests, point towards a pot of value. Value that you may not realise exists.

In a solo business, the *mastercraftspeople* may have very particular knowledge – intellectual property that others value and will pay for. A design that can be patented; a process that can be documented.

Similarly, the *freedom fighter* may possess a valuable model of business that can be replicated, franchised or licensed, and the *mountain climber* might have a drive and passion that is irresistible for an investor or attractive to an equally energetic climber.

The point is, value exists in every viable business. It might be your database, your client base, your physical base or your intellectual property. Your challenge is to start looking for and nailing the value.

While you may not have planned your exit from the beginning, it's never too late to start, and the knowledge you'll gain can't help but clarify your options.

But heed this little warning. If you've ever sold a house or sold a car, you'll be familiar with the excitement of 'the new' – the next house, the next car. If you're not careful, when you think too deeply about cashing in on your business, you might start to love what you've got right now a little less. And as we know, an unloved business is not attractive, to you or anyone else.

Exiting a business well can take many years of planning and execution. Love the one you're with right to the very end.

WHERE MAY YOUR VALUE LIE?

Having read this section, spend some time thinking about where the value in your business lies, or is likely to lie in the future.

Conclusion

I remember the moment it hit me that I simply *had* to do my own thing. It was some way through watching *Wild at Heart,* a 1990 arthouse gem from David Lynch.

Choice hurtled to compulsion.

In the movie, Nicholas Cage emerges from prison to be greeted by his glamourpuss girlfriend in a 1960s Ford Thunderbird convertible. It's that kind of movie.[1]

But it wasn't the car, the gum-chewing Laura Dern, or the end of incarceration that did it for him. It was the fact she'd remembered his treasured snakeskin jacket.

'Thanks, baby! Did I ever tell you that this here jacket represents a symbol of my individuality and my belief in personal freedom?'

---

1   Put 'Wild at Heart, snakeskin jacket' into YouTube's search bar and you'll find the clip. If that's not enough, try cranking up 'I'm free', recorded by the Rolling Stones in 1965. Better still, do both.

As it turns out, yes, he had told her before. Many thousands of times, as it goes. And at the time of writing, he's run up a similar count with me.

Barely a day goes by that I don't rejoice in my personal freedoms and celebrate my individuality.

While I want that for you too, I'm not expecting the same movie scene to talk to you as it did me. I get that different things resonate with different people.

But as you near the end of *The 1 Minute Commute*, my hope is that I have contributed in some way to your fresh view of the world of work. And if you're more assured that a life of soloism awaits, then my work is complete.

Except happily, it isn't. And may it never stop.

Similarly, I trust that your path to soloism doesn't end or stall here, but instead starts or reinvigorates from this moment on.

As I said in my introduction, I'd like to think you come back to *The 1 Minute Commute* time and again, that it becomes your user manual.

And to repeat myself further . . . working for yourself need not, and should not, mean working by yourself. Enjoy the brisk walk from your kitchen to the study, yes. But we soloists dominate the business landscape and will always benefit from the sharing of ideas, tips and stories.

In this book, I've told you what I know up to this point and I won't be stopping any day soon. Lots to learn, lots to share.

Enjoy your journey.

Acknowledgements

Writing a book takes time, and even one on the topic of working solo relies on a team of supporters.

Much of my creative writing time became available thanks to the generosity of my (recently) ex-business partners, Samantha Leader and Peter Crocker. For 12 wonderful years I had the pleasure of working alongside Sam and Peter and loved their company in a way that feels a bit weird. I'm not sure work colleagues are supposed to get along so well and have *that* much fun.

If there was a secret to our successful union I'd say it was that we never stopped behaving like a little collective of soloists, each striving to create something meaningful. They taught me masses about business, heaps about partnering and a fair bit about life. And yes, I shamelessly stole all their ideas for *The 1 Minute Commute.* They'd expect nothing less.

My relationship with my publisher, Pan Macmillan, has been equally pleasurable. From the moment Ingrid Ohlsson called me to say she'd be pleased to publish my book I have felt supported and directed by a team of artisans.

As my editor, I couldn't have wished for a better champion than Alex Lloyd, who from our first meeting showed himself to be someone who cares deeply about the books he helps birth. And when it comes to manuscript finessing, can there be anyone finer than Sam Sainsbury? I think not.

Finally, for their daily dose of inspiration I am indebted to my astonishingly resilient sister Jill; my gorgeous, creative wife Jane; my soul-full son Jay and, of course, the members of Australia's biggest community of little businesses.

To everyone, love *your* work.

Sources

Throughout *The 1 Minute Commute* I reference the numerous studies and polls undertaken with members of Flying Solo. Read all past studies here: www.flyingsolo.com.au/survey.

xv. One such resource was Mihaly Csikszentmihalyi's 2004 TED talk . . .: Mihaly Csikszentmihalyi, 'Flow, the secret to happiness', *TED*, February 2004, www.ted.com.

26. In a study by the California Energy Commission . . .: California Energy Commission, 'Windows and Offices: A Study of Office Worker Performance and the Indoor Environment', October 2003, www.energy.ca.gov.

28. A Harvard Business Review study found that a clean desk . . .: Boyoun (Grace) Chae and Rui (Juliet) Zhu, 'Why a Messy Workspace Undermines Your Persistence', *Harvard Business Review*, January 2015, hbr.org.

29. Try not to have a door behind you . . .: Go with Harmony, 'Use Feng Shui desk position tips to maximize your salary and career success', www.gowithharmony.com.
    (Tip: Explore the rules of Feng Shui. This resource has a good summary of how to set up your office to aid success.)

30. Studies have shown that . . .: Alpa V. Patel, Leslie Berstein et al, 'Leisure Time Spent Sitting in Relation to Total Mortality in a Prospective Cohort of US Adults', *American Journal of Epidemiology*, 2010, 172 (4), 2010, pp. 419–29.

30. The American Cancer Society . . .: Ariana Eunjung Cha, 'Standing for at least a quarter of the day reduces odds of obesity, new study finds', *The Washington Post*, November 2015.

47. Research undertaken by Hal Hershfield . . .: Alina Tugend, 'Bad Habits? My Future Self Will Deal With That', *The New York Times*, February 2012.

48. I'll finish with another fascinating finding . . .: Derek Thompson, 'Can Your Language Influence Your Spending, Eating, and Smoking Habits?', *The Atlantic*, September 2013; M. Keith Chen, 'The Effect of Language on Economic Behavior: Evidence from Savings Rates, Health Behaviors, and Retirement Assets', *American Economic Review*, 2013, 103(2): pp. 690–731.

57. Dan Pink has written a score of bestsellers . . .: Daniel H. Pink, *Drive*, Riverhead Books, New York City, 2011.

57. You may have seen his accompanying TED talk . . .: Dan Pink, 'The puzzle of motivation', *TED*, July 2009, https://www.ted.com.

62. That's from Ricky Gervais . . .: Alison Beard, 'Life's Work: Ricky Gervais', *Harvard Business Review*, April 2011, hbr.org.

69. Researchers from Stanford . . .: May Wong, 'Stanford study finds walking improves creativity', *Stanford News*, April 2014, news.stanford.edu; Marily Oppezzo and Daniel L. Schwartz, 'Give Your Ideas Some Legs: The Positive Effect of Walking on Creative Thinking', *Journal of Experimental Psychology: Learning, Memory, and Cognition*, 2014, Vol. 40, No. 4, pp. 1142–52, www.apa.org.

69. A study from the University of Notre Dame . . .: Gabriel Radvansky, 'Walking through doorways causes forgetting, new research shows', *Notre Dame News*, November 2011, news.nd.edu.

72. CB Insights in New York ran some research . . .: Erin Griffith, 'Why startups fail, according to their founders', *Fortune*, September 2014, fortune.com

72. The startling finding was that . . .: CB Insights, '242 Startup Failure Post-Mortems', October 2017, www.cbinsights.com.

74. Most small businesses don't fail . . .: Australian Small Business and Family Enterprise Ombudsman, 'Small Business Counts: Small Business in the Australian Economy', *Commonwealth of Australia*, 2016, p.20, www. asbfeo.gov.au; Peter Switzer, 'Exploding the myth of SME failure rates', *The Australian*, October 2007.

110. There's a great deal written on this topic . . .: Seth Godin, *Tribes*, Piatkus Books Ltd, London, 2008.

129. Research has shown that videos are 12 times . . .: William Arruda, 'Why You Need To Excel At Video', *Forbes*, June 2016, www.forbes.com.

132. Here's an important point to bear in mind . . .: Charles Arthur, 'What is the 1% rule?', *The Guardian*, July 2006.

134. Oxford University in England is one of the world's

leading . . .: Atlas Obscura, 'Oak Beams, New College Oxford', www.atlasobscura.com; Shawn Callahan, 'The Beams of New College, Oxford', *Anecdote*, January 2008, www.anecdote.com.

137. Just read Dr Robert Cialdini's groundbreaking book . . .: Robert B. Cialdini, PH.D., *Influence: The Psychology of Persuasion*, revised edition, Harper Business, 2006.

144. Richard Branson is a great supporter . . .: Richard Branson, *Business Stripped Bare*, Virgin Books, London, 2010.

144. Finally, before we explore tangible ways . . .: Andrew Blackman, 'Can Money Buy You Happiness?', *The Wall Street Journal*, November 2014.

158. One of the key findings . . .: Neil Rackham, *Spin Selling*, McGraw-Hill, London, 1988.

161. Research undertaken by the academic . . .: Kristen Le Mesurier, 'Indifference – a killer of business', *The Sydney Morning Herald*, February 2009.

166. Research carried out by . . .: USC Dornsife, 'To Multitask or Not to Multitask', *University of Southern California*, appliedpsychology.usc.edu; Vanessa Loder, 'Why Multi-Tasking Is Worse Than Marijuana For Your IQ', *Forbes*, June 2014, www.forbes.com.

166. In another study from the University of Sussex . . .: Jacqui Bealing, 'Brain scans reveal "grey matter" differences in media multitaskers', *PLOS One*, September 2014, www.sussex.ac.uk; Kep Kee Loh and Ryota Kanai, 'High media multi-tasking is associated with smaller gray-matter density in the anterior cingulate cortex', *PLOS One*, September 2014, http://journals.plos.org/plosone/article?id=10.1371/journal.pone.0106698.

166. Since the early 1990s 'cyber-slacking' . . .: Jennifer A. A. Lavoie and Timothy A. Pychyl, 'Cyberslacking and the Procrastination Superhighway', *SAGE Journals*, 2001, Vol. 19, issue 4, pp. 431–44, journals.sagepub.com.

169. Stephen Covey came up with another cracker . . .: Stephen R. Covey, *First Things First*, Free Press, New York, 1993.

173. I'm a strong advocate for assigning . . .: Cirillo Company, 'The Pomodoro Technique', cirillocompany.de.

180. Research by Gabriele Oettingen's psychology lab . . .: Gabriele Oettingen, 'The Problem With Positive Thinking', *The New York Times*, October 2014; Toni Bernhard J.D., 'Mental Contrasting: A Smart Alternative to Positive Thinking', *Psychology Today*, January 2015, www.psychologytoday.com.

204. That's a quote from . . .: Timothy Ferriss, *The 4-Hour Work Week*, Crown Publishing Group, New York, 2007.

212. Specific approval and feedback has been proven . . .: Brian Brim and Jim Asplund, 'Driving Engagement by Focusing on Strengths', *Gallup News*, November 2009, news.gallup.com.

215. For quite a while I've made use . . .: 16Personalities, www.16personalities.com.

230. Actions like these open up new pathways . . .: Carol Dweck, 'The power of believing that you can improve', *TED*, November 2014, www.ted.com.

235. The term 'service recovery paradox' . . .: C. de Matos, J. Henrique and C. Alberto Vargas Rossi, 'Service Recovery Paradox: A Meta-Analysis', *Journal of Service Research*, 2007, 10(1), pp. 60–77.

241. In *Built to Sell* . . .: John Warrillow, *Built to Sell*, Portfolio, New York, 2012.

Subscribe to Robert's show, *Mellow Brick Road*,
from wherever you get your podcasts.